VALUE INVESTING LOGBOOK

Journal Your Stock Investing Ideas so You Never Miss Out on a 10-Bagger Again

© Copyright Freeman Publications 2020 - All rights reserved.

The content contained within this book may not be reproduced, duplicated or transmitted without direct written permission from the author or the publisher.

Under no circumstances will any blame or legal responsibility be held against the publisher, or author, for any damages, reparation, or monetary loss due to the information contained within this book, either directly or indirectly.

Legal Notice:

This book is copyright protected. It is only for personal use. You cannot amend, distribute, sell, use, quote or paraphrase any part, or the content within this book, without the consent of the author or publisher.

Disclaimer Notice:

The following work is presented for informational purposes only. None of the information herein constitutes an offer to sell or buy any security or investment vehicle, nor does it constitute an investment recommendation of a legal, tax, accounting or investment recommendation by Freeman Publications, its employees or paid contributors. The information is presented without regard for individual investment preferences or risk parameters and is general, non-tailored, non-specific information.

Freeman Publications, including all employees and paid contributors, agree not to trade in any security they write about for a minimum of three days (72 hours) following publication of a new article, book, report or email. Except for existing orders that were in place before submission (any such orders will also always be disclosed inside the document). This includes equity, options, debt, or other instruments directly related to that security, stock, or company. The author may have indirect positions in some companies mentioned due to holdings in mutual funds, ETFs, Closed End Funds or other similar vehicles, and there is no guarantee that the author is aware of the individual portfolios of any of those funds at any given time. Such indirect holdings will generally not be disclosed.

Warning:

There is no magic formula to getting rich, in the financial markets or otherwise. Investing often involves high risks and you can lose a lot of money. Success in investment vehicles with the best prospects for price appreciation can only be achieved through proper and rigorous research and analysis. Please do not invest with money you cannot afford to lose. The opinions in this content are just that, opinions of the authors. We are a publishing company and the opinions, comments, stories, reports, advertisements and articles we publish are for informational and educational purposes only; nothing herein should be considered personalized investment advice. Before you make any investment, check with your investment professional (advisor). We urge our readers to review the financial statements and prospectus of any company they are interested in. We are not responsible for any damages or losses arising from the use of any information herein. Past performance is not a guarantee of future results.

This work is based on SEC filings, current events, interviews, corporate press releases, and what we've learned as financial journalists. It may contain errors and you shouldn't make any investment decision based solely on what you read here. It is your money and your responsibility.

Freeman Publications Ltd. are 100% independent in that we are not affiliated with any security, investment vehicle, bank or brokerage house.

All registered trademarks are the property of their respective owners.

WHY USE A LOGBOOK?

Management guru Peter Drucker once said, "[only] what gets measured, gets managed."

And when it comes to investing in stocks, we found one of the biggest reasons investors weren't getting results is that they didn't have a consistent process for selecting them in the first place.

Sometimes they would buy off a tip from a friend or family member.

Other times they would hear about a company in a Facebook Group, or on a website trying to sell them a $2,000 stock newsletter subscription.

They would then select them based on arbitrary criteria, like being in a particular industry, or paying a dividend over 5%.

Now if you've done this in the past, don't worry.

There are very few people on Earth who can say they haven't.

That's where this logbook comes in because using it will benefit you for two main reasons.

1. Help you overcome your own biases.

By being able to spot patterns in your investing, you'll be able to evolve and iterate your process.

Perhaps you're looking at companies without a competitive advantage or moat. Or ones that don't have any recurring revenue built into their business model.

That's why we included our checklist to see for yourself how many of our successful company criteria each company meets.

2. Track your actions. How long do you wait before buying a stock?

Price anchoring is a massive obstacle that many investors struggle with. We'll cover it in more depth in the next few pages, but for now, ask yourself this.

Have you ever discovered a stock, decided not to invest, and then a few days later, the price goes up by 10%?

So you hold off buying, hoping for a dip. But that dip never comes, and before you know it, the stock is up 30 or 40%.

Or on the flipside. How many times have you bought a stock at what turned out to be the highest price possible... only to see the stock go lower right after you bought it?

The funny thing is, this doesn't happen as often as you think it does.

But you DO remember the times when it does happen.

That's why this book exists.

Because by tracking how you select stocks, you will understand why your best stocks are performing the way they are.

So you can buy more companies like these great stocks, while avoiding money losing duds along the way.

No one gets it right 100% of the time. So you shouldn't expect yourself to

Legendary investor Peter Lynch, who achieved some of the best returns ever for a fund manager (29.2% annual growth over a 13 year period), said that you only need to be right 6/10 times when investing.

Because your winners, provided you hold them for a long time, will always make up for any losers.

HOW TO USE THIS BOOK

The concept here is simple. Whenever you find a company that you're interested in, fill out each field of the logbook.

Some are self-explanatory, such as the company name, industry, and ticker symbol.

Others, like the current price and the 52 week high/low prices, are designed to help you see the company in the context of the bigger picture. Is this company on the rise, has it been beaten down heavily over the past year?

Then we have our 10 criteria, which every successful company meets. The most important thing to remember with these criteria is that a successful company DOES NOT have to complete all 10. A young company that is growing at a fast pace, is unlikely to have the best cash position because all funds are being re-invested to achieve more growth.

The same goes for a more mature business. Just because there have been some leadership changes lately, doesn't necessarily mean the company is no good.

So with these criteria, the more, the better. If a company has all 10, then that's fantastic. If it only has 8 or 9, then don't count it out, but study why it is missing specific criteria.

If a company meets 7 or less, it's a good sign that you should stay away.

The final part of the analysis are some basic financial numbers. These can all be found for free on websites like Yahoo Finance, and in the next few pages, we'll show you exactly where to find them.

The point with only using basic numbers is not to make things too complicated. Entire college level courses have been taught on how to value a company. And searching for "how to value a company" brings you down an endless rabbit hole of different models, formulas and calculations.

We like to take a more straightforward approach, based on a quote by Warren Buffett.

"It is better to be approximately correct than precisely wrong."

So in this section, you simply note the Price to Earnings (PE) ratio or the Price to Sales (PS) ratio for a company that isn't yet profitable. As well as the projected growth rate for the next 5 years.

This is so you get a feel for the different ways companies are priced at different stages of their lifecycle.

For example, right now, Tesla has a PE ratio of over 1,000. No, that's not a typo. It's 1,120 at the time of writing. However, a group of 17 analysts project Tesla's growth at around 300% per year (again, not a typo) over the next 5 years.

Johnson & Johnson, on the other hand, has a more reasonable PE ratio of 22.64. But has a far lower projected annual growth rate of 4.38% over the next 5 years.

This doesn't mean one company is a better investment than the other (although we're sure anyone who owns Tesla in 2020 could make a compelling argument).

But it does illustrate how the market values different companies based on projected growth.

Now we've covered the numbers, let's expand on the more qualitative aspects of the business.

SUMMARY OF THE FREEMAN CRITERIA FOR A SUCCESSFUL COMPANY

This is a condensed version of our full Rational Process Investing methodology that we cover inside our bestselling book The 8 Step Beginner's Guide to Value Investing. If you would like to learn more about our methodology, as well as discover 20 great companies which meet this criteria today, then the book is available on Kindle, Paperback and Audiobook on Amazon.com.

Where you first heard about the company is as crucial as when you heard about it

Sometimes becoming a more profitable investor is a case of being able to filter your information, and knowing who to pay attention to.

For example, did you first hear about a company as a stock tip from a friend?

Did you see someone post about it in a Facebook Group, or on Twitter?

Did Jim Cramer shout from the rooftops that this was a "CAN'T MISS PROSPECT"

These are usually signs that you should take their advice with a grain of salt unless your friend has an excellent track record in the market.

On the other hand, one of our favorite ways of hearing about a company is by asking ourselves this question.

Did some talk about the company before they mentioned the stock?

This is usually a good sign because behind every great stock is a great company.

To give a personal anecdote, this is how we first heard about Peloton.

One of our friends couldn't stop talking about how much they loved their Peloton bike and how they'd stopped going to their local spin classes because of it. This was the catalyst to start our research where we fell in love with the business model and how the company was marketing itself. The stock is up roughly 120% since we first purchased it.

We're not using this example to brag, but to demonstrate that great stocks often begin with someone talking about how great the company is, rather than how great the stock is.

Do You Understand the Business?

This is, by far the most important criteria. If you don't understand what a company does, you shouldn't own the stock. It's that simple.

Your Unique Advantage

Everyone has a unique advantage in this regard.

Someone who works in digital advertising is far more likely

to understand a company like The Trade Desk than a retailer like AutoZone.

But someone who has been an AutoZone employee for 15 years will have an edge on understanding how the company works vs. anyone, including Wall Street pros.

A good test for this is what we call **The 3 Sentence Test**.

Can you explain what the company does and how it makes money in 3 sentences or less? If not, you probably don't understand it well enough.

It's also important to distinguish between the surface level business the company is in and their bottom line profits. For example, McDonald's might be a "fast food company," but the real money is made in its real estate business and franchise model.

The fast food business is just a catalyst for this. McDonald's owns the real estate on which all its restaurants are built. The company then turns around and leases the stores to its franchisees and charges them rent that is well above market price.

They can do this because the McDonald's brand is so strong (which we'll talk more about in the intangible assets section), meaning franchisees are willing to pay a premium on rent.

Another example of a business that is seemingly another line of business is Starbucks. Many naysayers have been saying for years that Starbucks is an overpriced coffee chain. However, people who truly understand Starbucks know that while the company is a coffee chain, it's really in the "third space" business.

What Starbucks is selling is not coffee, but a place you can spend time that isn't your home or office. It is where people meet one another for informal meetings, catch up, and go on dates. It is a convenient place to work from as well, given the rising number of remote workers. It's also considered a premium product, but one which is available at an affordable price point.

Many Starbucks naysayers will laugh at the idea of paying $5 for a cup of coffee, but if Starbucks' customer base thought this way, they would have gone bankrupt in the 1980s. Instead, the stock has risen 900% over the past decade.

Is the Business in a Growing or Stable Sector?

This one is relatively simple; you want to buy companies that are either on the way up or already stable. You don't want to buy ones that are on the way down. Blockbuster might have been a good investment in the 1980s, not so much in 2008. The same goes for non-specialist retail stores in the mid-2010s, when Amazon took the lion's share of the general retail business.

Does it Have an Intangible Asset Advantage?

This criteria is also known as "what you won't find on the balance sheet".

A company has two types of assets: Tangible and intangible. A building or a factory is a tangible asset, as are the goods that the company produces. These are easily quantifiable. Intangible assets aren't so easy, to the point where it's often impossible to put a numerical value on them.

For example, Coca-Cola has one of the most significant intangible assets in the world: Its trademark. The phrase "Coca-Cola" is recognizable all around the world. If we were to pour Coca-Cola into another bottle and call it "Freeman Cola," would you drink it? Even if it tastes the same as Coca-Cola, you'll be unlikely to switch your preference to the new drink. This is the power of an intangible asset.

Ferrari is another company that has a similar pull. Swap the badge on a Ferrari with anything else, and people will suddenly want to pay far less for it, even if it is in the right shade of scarlet. The best companies have some form of intangible assets that work for them. This could be a brand name, a patent, or a process that gives them a competitive advantage in the marketplace.

Management quality is also a critical intangible asset. For example, Apple under Steve Jobs had one of the biggest intangible assets that could not be quantified on their financial statement. The same goes for Tesla today, with Elon Musk at the helm.

Disney is another example of a company with significant intangible assets in the form of over 90 years of intellectual property.

One often-overlooked intangible asset is the company's employees. Not in terms of the number of them, or their average salary, but how much people want to work for the company. It's no surprise that a company like Google has an average of 428 applicants for every open job position. A good way to gauge this is to go on Glassdoor.com, a website where employees can anonymously grade their employer and check out the company's average rating.

Does it Have a Moat?

This is a term Warren Buffett uses frequently when speaking of what he looks for in businesses to invest in. Internally, when one of our team brings up a new company to look into, our first question is often, "is there a moat?".

An economic moat is some condition that gives a company a significant competitive advantage. It could be anything from size to trademarks and patents or a business process.

For example, Amazon's size offers it a considerable economic moat. The company offers customers bargain-basement level prices, and it's able to do this thanks to its sheer size. Its average cost per unit is far lower than what a smaller retailer can offer, and thus, Amazon can afford to earn a small percentage of profit, but it sells so much of it that the amount of profit it earns is high.

Coca-Cola has a strong economic moat through its brand name. Everyone recognizes it, and everyone buys it because of that. Interestingly, Berkshire Hathaway, Buffett's investment vechicle, has significant holdings in both Amazon and Coca-Cola as well as Apple, another company with a strong brand moat.

Another factor that can create a moat is one we've seen the power of recently, namely a large number of users. For example, Google and Facebook are popular thanks to the large number of users they have. This is an example of a moat caused by the network effect. Network effect happens when companies build a significant userbase, which provides a better customer experience, leading to an even higher number of users.

Facebook is a perfect example of this. There comes a tipping point in many people's lives where not using Facebook is more detrimental to their quality of life than using it. All of this creates a better user experience for the people on the platform and fuels more growth. We see similar examples in the workspace communication space with companies like Slack and Zoom.

Other examples of moats are companies operating in non-sexy industries. Non-sexy industries are great because companies receive less analyst attention, they are less prone to disruption, and the incumbents can often have a natural monopoly.

A great example of this is Waste Management. You don't have to be a genius to figure out which industry the company is in. Now imagine being an employee of Waste Management. If you met someone at a BBQ, would you introduce yourself as your job title "I work in marketing," or would you let them know you work for a company called Waste Management.
In addition, there aren't too many 20somethings in Silicon Valley spending all night hyped up on caffeine and Adderall hypothesizing on how to disrupt the waste management industry. That is a big reason why the stock is up 400% in the past decade.

Another factor that can cause a moat is a company operating in a morally or ethically dubious industry. Tobacco, alcohol, and casino companies all fall under this category.

We should note that you should never compromise your moral or ethical views just to make money. The beauty of long term investing is that you can eliminate pretty much any industry you don't want to invest in but still make a killing in sectors which do fit within your views or beliefs

Does it Have Strong Management?

It isn't easy to evaluate the quality of management. Most shareholders look at the stock price and then reverse engineer whether management is any good. This is a bit like looking at the quality of windows in a house and figuring out whether it's a good investment. There's a lot more to it than just that!

One of the most prominent qualities you need to look for in management is its ability to adapt. For example, Kodak was one of the biggest companies in the photography space, thanks to its development film business. When the digital revolution came, it doubled down on film and is now just an afterthought.

The development of the smartphone, in turn, left many digital camera producing companies in the dust. Some pivoted successfully to making high-end cameras for professionals (Canon, GoPro) while others never quite made the leap (Vivitar).

It often comes down to honesty. Honesty in communications is one half of this. How willing is management to disclose the business conditions to shareholders in their reports? Are they willing to admit faults and mistakes?

The Management's Discussion and Analysis (MD&A) section of the company's financial reports provides a good read on how honest management is. Reading prior reports and looking at how management evaluated the business environment is a good way to get a handle on how they tend to communicate and view conditions.

An excellent example of this was Jeff Bezos' letters to shareholders when Amazon was still a fledgling company. Bezos constantly reiterated his vision for the business and did not focus on minutia, like whether they hit a Wall Street analyst's earnings estimates for the last quarter. This is the kind of long-term thinking you want to see from management.

On the flip side, we have examples of CEOs believing their own hype. While it wasn't a public company, the saga of Theranos' Elizabeth Holmes is instructive. While Holmes has a large list of faults, almost all of her conduct stems from the fact that she could not be honest with herself about what the company could deliver in a reasonable timeline.

Two public examples of this, which both ended terribly for investors, were Enron, and more recently, Luckin Coffee. In both cases, there was a systemic culture of management fabricating sales numbers. Sadly for investors, both stocks plunged over 95% from their highs. In the case of Enron, this resulted in what was at the time, the largest corporate bankruptcy in history.

Are Company Insiders Buying the Stock?

This is one of our "secret weapons" when it comes to investing.

No one should know more about a company's prospects than its board of directors. Well, fortunately, due to Section 403 of the Sarbanes-Oxley Act (which was designed to make corporations more transparent), directors, officers, and principal shareholders, must, by law, declare any stock purchases or sales within 2 trading days.

When management owns the stock, it's a sign that their interest lies with the shareholders... <u>because they are the shareholders.</u>

This is why company insiders buying shares is a fantastic sign for the company's short and long-term prospects. And the more insiders who are buying, the better.

To find this information 20 years ago, you would have had to scour various newspapers or call your broker and have them send you a report in the mail. In 2021, it's never been easier to get your hands on this. You can do it for free online, and in the next chapter, we'll show you exactly where to look.

Does it Have Recurring Revenue?

Recurring revenue has shifted from a "nice to have" to a must. We've seen many industries move from an ownership model where you pay a lump sum upfront, to a rental model where you keep paying a small fee every month to access the service.

Every single one of the largest companies in the world has recurring revenue built into their business model.

Amazon not only has recurring revenue in the form of subscription services like Amazon Prime, Audible, and Twitch. It also has recurring revenue in its Amazon Web Services (AWS) division, the most profitable company.

Companies like Apple have recurring revenue because consumers usually buy a new iPhone or iPad every 2-3 years, and then a new Macbook every 3-4 years. Apple doesn't have to spend much on marketing to get existing customers to buy, because once they're in, they're usually in for life.

We're now seeing recurring revenue seep into industries you wouldn't have thought of. Tesla for example, now charges users a monthly fee for "Premium Connectivity" in their cars. Nike has implemented a subscription service for kids' shoes. HP now has a subscription service set up which auto-orders more ink cartridges for your printer when ink runs low.

The best recurring revenue models benefit both the consumer and the company. So ensure the company you are looking at ticks this box.

Are its Earnings Growing?

We always want to see company earnings trending one way, and that's upwards. Even if a company is not yet profitable, we at least want to see revenue rising. We like to look at this over 5 years if possible, but if the company is still young, then a shorter period is acceptable.

We should note that with the current economic conditions, it's likely that many companies will have their 2020 earnings numbers affected. It's up to you to decide whether this is a temporary blip or a permanent change in the economics of the company you are researching.

If it's the former, then continue your research. However, if the pandemic has shifted the company's business model in a way you don't believe they will be able to recover from, then stay well away.

Does it Have a Healthy Cash Position?

Cash is the lifeblood of any company. Without it, no company can survive.

When we speak of a cash position, we refer specifically to the company's level of cash relative to its expenses and liabilities. A stable cash position allows a company to cover its current liabilities with a combination of cash and liquid assets.

A large cash position is a symbol of financial strength, but too large is often sign that management is poor at managing capital. The exceptions to this are companies like Berkshire Hathaway and Markel, who use their cash reserves to capitalize on acquisition opportunities.

This is also why recessions destroy companies built solely on debt, whereas companies who maintain healthy cash reserves (like Berkshire Hathaway) can ride the wave through to the other side.

Can it Weather a Storm?

The final point we like to consider is how robust a company's business model is. Can it withstand a stress test? Stress tests are scenarios where analysts project profitability numbers based on the assumption of adverse conditions.

For example, a hotel chain is unlikely to survive an 60% vacancy rate for too long before things get ugly. Airlines are also notorious for their inability to handle the slightest disruption to their business conditions.

For every business, a standard stress test is a reduction in sales. The higher the business's ability to withstand this stress, the safer your investment will be. Another example of a stress test is multiple Acts of God in quick succession for the insurance industry.

Another point to note here is if a large portion of a company's revenue comes from a single product, supplier, or contract, the company now has a single point of failure. This makes it susceptible to catastrophe is this point of failure is tested.

GT Advanced Technology is the best example of this in recent years. The company made the headlines after being chosen as the screen supplier for the early editions of the iPhone. However, when Apple switched to a different supplier for the iPhone 6, the companies fortunes were wrecked. The Apple contract made up almost 80% of the total revenue for the glass manufacturer, who eventually filed for bankruptcy after shares fell by more than 90% in a few days.

WHY WE INCLUDED FUTURE STOCK PRICES

We also decided to include a field that some of you may find unusual. Namely, the price of the stock after you first heard about it.

This section was inspired by a thread we wrote on Twitter (follow us @CEOFreeman) of all places.

It ended up getting a lot of traction, including the attention of David Gardner, co-founder of the fantastic Investment company *The Motley Fool*.

We included the future price in the future because some people look at a company's stock price and decide it's too expensive. So they never buy shares in the company at all. Others may buy a few shares, but never add to their initial position, even after a stock has proven itself by producing exceptional returns.

We've all done it.

Why?

Because our brains are hard-wired to plant a big obstacle in our path to financial freedom, what's the obstacle?

It's called Price Anchoring.

Price anchoring is part of a broader phenomenon called Anchoring Bias.

Where your brain gets distracted by information you connect with something you're thinking about, even when that information isn't relevant at all to the original thought. In sales, you see price anchoring all the time.

It's why every single e-commerce website puts the RRP before the actual sale price.

By first seeing a higher price, you get anchored to that price (like in the above examples)

So when you see the lower price, it makes you think you're getting a bargain. This happens even if you completely understand why companies are doing this.

Now in stock investing, the opposite happens.

You get anchored to a lower price, and this kills your returns.

Because there are two numbers you're anchored to when deciding whether to buy a stock.

The first is the price at which you first heard about a stock.

This one applies if you've never invested in the stock before.

The second applies if you already own shares. It's the price you first bought the stock at.

When stocks go above your anchor price, it's harder to buy shares. So you stay on the sidelines and make excuses for not investing. While hoping the stock falls back to your anchor price.

Why is price anchoring so hard to overcome? Because we're trained to look for bargains.

So when a stock price is at an all-time high. You feel like you're getting ripped off. Especially compared to your anchor price.

Plus, we hate losing.

As humans, we act more to avoid a potential loss, than we will to make potential gains (survival instinct)

Because the amount of pain that loss causes is far greater than the amount of happiness, you get from potential profits.

How many times have you bought a stock at what turned out to be the highest price possible, only to see the stock go lower right after you bought it?

The funny thing is, this doesn't happen as often as you think it does. But you DO remember the times when it does happen.

Price anchoring can be devastating to your long-term results.

Because anchoring will likely prevent you from benefitting from the stocks that go up the most.

Even Warren Buffett isn't immune from this…

Buffett started buying Wal-Mart in the 90s. But when the stock inched pennies above his $11.50 target price, he stopped adding to his position. The stock only went up after and it's now worth $150 per share. Buffett estimates he missed out on $10 billion by not buying more.

Just think about huge winners like Amazon, Tesla, Zoom and NVIDIA. Think of how much it would cost to miss out on 1,000%+ gains because you did not want to pay a few extra cents per share. Then think about the cost of not adding to those positions over time.

How to beat it.

You will never fully eliminate price anchoring from your investment decisions. But there are some ways you can reduce its impact. And that's why we included the price boxes in your logbook.

Note down the prices after you first heard about the company.

First it will show you that not every company shoots to the moon if you don't invest.

Second, it will show you that you don't always buy at the top. On top of this, if you're struggling with investing into a company, the easiest way is to split your initial investment into thirds. Buy 1/3 today, 1/3 in 30 days, and 1/3 in 60 days, regardless of price.

So don't let price anchoring keep you from buying an outstanding stock. Or adding more shares to a current winner.

WHERE TO FIND THE NUMBERS

As we mentioned before, it's never been easier to find all the necessary information about a company.

What used to take weeks now takes minutes.

And best of all, you can find out everything you need to know for free.

Our favorite resource for getting a snapshot of a company's financial data is Yahoo Finance.

You can by going to https://finance.yahoo.com and typing in the company name in the search bar.

This will bring up this screen.

From here, you can see we get the following information

- Current price - $231.55
- Market Cap - $542.97 Billion
- 52 week high - $234.99
- 52 week low - $159.50

- Dividend – N/A (Berkshire Hathaway does not pay a dividend)
- PE Ratio – 15.63 (Note: We took this from the BRK.A data. Always take PE ratio from a company's A class shares)

If the company you're researching isn't yet profitable, the PE ratio on the screen will display as N/A. For these companies you will need to find the Price to Sales ratio, which is located on the Statistics tab as Price/sales (ttm).

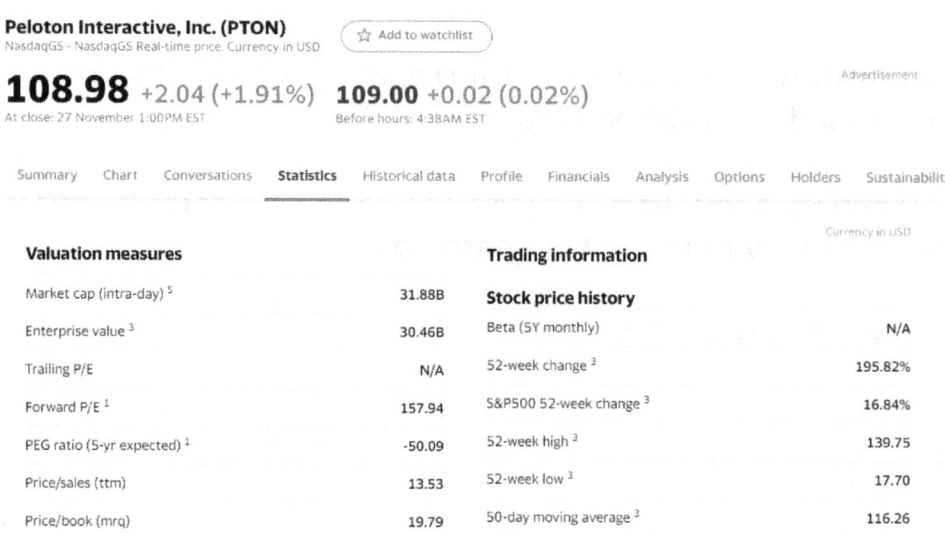

Now we can find some other numbers by clicking on the various tabs. The first number we will find is the projected growth over the next 5 years. We see this by clicking on the analysis tab. Once you've clicked on the analysis tab, scroll down until you find the section titled **Growth Estimates**. From there, you can use the next 5 years (per annum) number.

Berkshire Hathaway Inc. (BRK-B)
NYSE - NYSE Delayed price. Currency in USD

231.55 -1.58 (-0.68%)
At close: 27 November 1:02PM EST

Summary Chart Conversations Statistics Historical data Profile Financials **Analysis** Options Holders Sustainability

Growth estimates	BRK-B	Industry	Sector(s)	S&P 500
Current qtr.	26.50%	N/A	N/A	N/A
Next qtr.	6.60%	N/A	N/A	N/A
Current year	-4.80%	N/A	N/A	N/A
Next year	16.80%	N/A	N/A	N/A
Next 5 years (per annum)	23.30%	N/A	N/A	N/A
Past 5 years (per annum)	N/A	N/A	N/A	N/A

As you can see from the above image, Berkshire Hathaway's projected growth rate over the next 5 years is 23.3% per year. The majority of this will come from their Apple holdings.

The final tab we will use is the Holders tab. We use this to find insider buying activity. Berkshire Hathaway didn't have any insider buying activity last year, so we used another company, Peloton, to demonstrate this.

Peloton Interactive, Inc. (PTON)
NasdaqGS - NasdaqGS Real-time price. Currency in USD

108.98 +2.04 (+1.91%)
At close: 27 November 1:00PM EST

Summary Chart Conversations Statistics Historical data Profile Financials Analysis Options **Holders** Sustainability

Major holders   Insider roster   **Insider transactions**

Insider transactions   Currency in USD

Insider purchases - Last 6 months	Shares	Trans
Purchases	31,248,611	33
Sales	1,718,584	22
Net shares purchased (sold)	29,530,027	55
Total insider shares held	2.71M	N/A
% net shares purchased (sold)	-110.10%	N/A

Once you are on the holders tab, click on the section titled **Insider Transactions**.

From the image, you can see that there were 33 purchase transactions and 22 sales over the past 6 months. But more importantly, there were almost 20x as many shares purchased by insiders as there were shares sold. This is a great sign and one that indicates Peloton has a strong future ahead of it.

Now you can fill in all the appropriate numbers in your logbook, and it will only take you 5 minutes at the most. In the logbook section, we've filled in a sample of this for Berkshire Hathaway, using the figures above so that you can see the finished product.

USING THE TRANSACTIONS SECTION

We've also included a transaction section where you can record your stock purchases or sales.

This is to reference how many of the stocks you research end up becoming stocks you own.

You can also see how long it takes you to act after finding an opportunity.

If you found a stock that met all ten criteria but then took six months to buy it, chances are you missed out on some fantastic gains.

On the other hand, if you bought a stock the same day you heard of it, without doing thorough research, chances are you made a loss.

All of this is with the sole goal of making you understand yourself at a deeper level, which will make you a better investor.

HOW TO 10X YOUR RESULTS FROM THIS BOOK IN 3 SIMPLE STEPS

STEP 1.

Get our Free Company Valuation 101 Video Course

In this 7 part video course, you'll discover our process for accurately valuing a company. This will help you determine if a stock is overvalued, correctly valued, or a bargain. Giving you an indicator of whether to buy or not.

Plus, you'll get 6 other exclusive bonus reports for free.

Get your course for free by going to
https://freemanpublications.com/bonus

Check out our other books

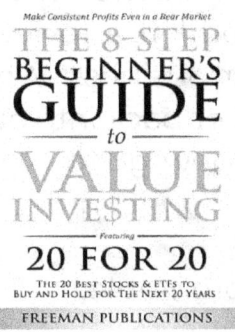

If you enjoyed this book and want to learn more about our investing methodology, including 20 stocks that meet our criteria. Then check out our bestselling book The 8 Step Beginner's Guide to Value Investing on Amazon.

The 20 stocks included outperformed the S&P 500 by 2:1 so far in 2020, and they show no signs of slowing down.

Connect with us on Social Media

We're not like the markets, because we never close.
Instead, we keep the conversation going 24/7/365 on social media.

Follow us on Twitter *@CEOFreeman*

Or join our free Facebook Group by going to
https://freemanpublications.com/facebook

Even if we don't see you inside the group, we wish you all the success in the world with your investments.

One final word from us. If this book has helped you in any way, we'd appreciate it if you left a review on Amazon. Reviews are the lifeblood of our business. We read every single one and incorporate your feedback into our future book projects. To leave an Amazon review, go to
https://freemanpublications.com/leaveareview

Stay healthy and stay profitable,

Freeman Publications

Investing Ideas

Company Name			Ticker Symbol		Industry		Current Market Cap		
Berkshire Hathaway			BRK.B		*Holding Company*		*$542 Billion*		
Date I First Heard About It		Where I first heard about it			Current Price		52 week high	52 week low	Current Dividend Yield
11/27/2020		*Interview with Warren Buffett*			$231.55		$234.99	$159.50	N/A
Under-stand the business	Grow-ing or Stable Industry	Intangible Asset Advantage	Moat	Strong Manage-ment	Insiders Are Buying	Recurring Revenue	Growing Earnings	Healthy Cash Position	Can It Weather a Storm?
√	√	√	√	√	×	√	√	√	√
PE Ratio	PS Ratio	Projected Rate Growth (5 years)			Price 30 days later	Price 60 days later	Price 90 days later	Price 180 days later	Price 1 year later
15.63		23.30%							

Notes

Company Name			Ticker Symbol		Industry		Current Market Cap		
Date I First Heard About It		Where I first heard about it			Current Price		52 week high	52 week low	Current Dividend Yield
Under-stand the business	Grow-ing or Stable Industry	Intangible Asset Advantage	Moat	Strong Manage-ment	Insiders Are Buying	Recurring Revenue	Growing Earnings	Healthy Cash Position	Can It Weather a Storm?
PE Ratio	PS Ratio	Projected Rate Growth (5 years)			Price 30 days later	Price 60 days later	Price 90 days later	Price 180 days later	Price 1 year later

Notes

Investing Ideas

Company Name		Ticker Symbol		Industry		Current Market Cap			
Date I First Heard About It		Where I first heard about it			Current Price		52 week high	52 week low	Current Dividend Yield
Under-stand the business	Grow-ing or Stable Industry	Intangible Asset Advantage	Moat	Strong Management	Insiders Are Buying	Recurring Revenue	Growing Earnings	Healthy Cash Position	Can It Weather a Storm?
PE Ratio	PS Ratio	Projected Rate Growth (5 years)			Price 30 days later	Price 60 days later	Price 90 days later	Price 180 days later	Price 1 year later

Notes

Company Name		Ticker Symbol		Industry		Current Market Cap			
Date I First Heard About It		Where I first heard about it			Current Price		52 week high	52 week low	Current Dividend Yield
Under-stand the business	Grow-ing or Stable Industry	Intangible Asset Advantage	Moat	Strong Management	Insiders Are Buying	Recurring Revenue	Growing Earnings	Healthy Cash Position	Can It Weather a Storm?
PE Ratio	PS Ratio	Projected Rate Growth (5 years)			Price 30 days later	Price 60 days later	Price 90 days later	Price 180 days later	Price 1 year later

Notes

Investing Ideas

Company Name			Ticker Symbol			Industry		Current Market Cap		

Date I First Heard About It	Where I first heard about it			Current Price		52 week high	52 week low	Current Dividend Yield

Under-stand the business	Grow-ing or Stable Industry	Intangible Asset Advantage	Moat	Strong Manage-ment	Insiders Are Buying	Recurring Revenue	Growing Earnings	Healthy Cash Position	Can It Weather a Storm?

PE Ratio	PS Ratio	Projected Rate Growth (5 years)		Price 30 days later	Price 60 days later	Price 90 days later	Price 180 days later	Price 1 year later

Notes

Company Name			Ticker Symbol			Industry		Current Market Cap		

Date I First Heard About It	Where I first heard about it			Current Price		52 week high	52 week low	Current Dividend Yield

Under-stand the business	Grow-ing or Stable Industry	Intangible Asset Advantage	Moat	Strong Manage-ment	Insiders Are Buying	Recurring Revenue	Growing Earnings	Healthy Cash Position	Can It Weather a Storm?

PE Ratio	PS Ratio	Projected Rate Growth (5 years)		Price 30 days later	Price 60 days later	Price 90 days later	Price 180 days later	Price 1 year later

Notes

Investing Ideas

Company Name			Ticker Symbol			Industry		Current Market Cap		

Date I First Heard About It	Where I first heard about it			Current Price		52 week high	52 week low	Current Dividend Yield

Understand the business	Growing or Stable Industry	Intangible Asset Advantage	Moat	Strong Management	Insiders Are Buying	Recurring Revenue	Growing Earnings	Healthy Cash Position	Can It Weather a Storm?

PE Ratio	PS Ratio	Projected Rate Growth (5 years)		Price 30 days later	Price 60 days later	Price 90 days later	Price 180 days later	Price 1 year later

Notes

Company Name			Ticker Symbol			Industry		Current Market Cap		

Date I First Heard About It	Where I first heard about it			Current Price		52 week high	52 week low	Current Dividend Yield

Understand the business	Growing or Stable Industry	Intangible Asset Advantage	Moat	Strong Management	Insiders Are Buying	Recurring Revenue	Growing Earnings	Healthy Cash Position	Can It Weather a Storm?

PE Ratio	PS Ratio	Projected Rate Growth (5 years)		Price 30 days later	Price 60 days later	Price 90 days later	Price 180 days later	Price 1 year later

Notes

Investing Ideas

Company Name		Ticker Symbol			Industry		Current Market Cap		

Date I First Heard About It	Where I first heard about it				Current Price		52 week high	52 week low	Current Dividend Yield

Under-stand the business	Grow-ing or Stable Industry	Intangible Asset Advantage	Moat	Strong Manage-ment	Insiders Are Buying	Recurring Revenue	Growing Earnings	Healthy Cash Position	Can It Weather a Storm?

PE Ratio	PS Ratio	Projected Rate Growth (5 years)			Price 30 days later	Price 60 days later	Price 90 days later	Price 180 days later	Price 1 year later

Notes

Company Name		Ticker Symbol			Industry		Current Market Cap		

Date I First Heard About It	Where I first heard about it				Current Price		52 week high	52 week low	Current Dividend Yield

Under-stand the business	Grow-ing or Stable Industry	Intangible Asset Advantage	Moat	Strong Manage-ment	Insiders Are Buying	Recurring Revenue	Growing Earnings	Healthy Cash Position	Can It Weather a Storm?

PE Ratio	PS Ratio	Projected Rate Growth (5 years)			Price 30 days later	Price 60 days later	Price 90 days later	Price 180 days later	Price 1 year later

Notes

Investing Ideas

Company Name		Ticker Symbol		Industry		Current Market Cap		

Date I First Heard About It	Where I first heard about it			Current Price	52 week high	52 week low	Current Dividend Yield

Under-stand the business	Grow-ing or Stable Industry	Intangible Asset Advantage	Moat	Strong Manage-ment	Insiders Are Buying	Recurring Revenue	Growing Earnings	Healthy Cash Position	Can It Weather a Storm?

PE Ratio	PS Ratio	Projected Rate Growth (5 years)		Price 30 days later	Price 60 days later	Price 90 days later	Price 180 days later	Price 1 year later

Notes

Company Name		Ticker Symbol		Industry		Current Market Cap		

Date I First Heard About It	Where I first heard about it			Current Price	52 week high	52 week low	Current Dividend Yield

Under-stand the business	Grow-ing or Stable Industry	Intangible Asset Advantage	Moat	Strong Manage-ment	Insiders Are Buying	Recurring Revenue	Growing Earnings	Healthy Cash Position	Can It Weather a Storm?

PE Ratio	PS Ratio	Projected Rate Growth (5 years)		Price 30 days later	Price 60 days later	Price 90 days later	Price 180 days later	Price 1 year later

Notes

Investing Ideas

Company Name		Ticker Symbol			Industry		Current Market Cap		

Date I First Heard About It	Where I first heard about it			Current Price			52 week high	52 week low	Current Dividend Yield

Under-stand the business	Grow-ing or Stable Industry	Intangible Asset Advantage	Moat	Strong Manage-ment	Insiders Are Buying	Recurring Revenue	Growing Earnings	Healthy Cash Position	Can It Weather a Storm?

PE Ratio	PS Ratio	Projected Rate Growth (5 years)			Price 30 days later	Price 60 days later	Price 90 days later	Price 180 days later	Price 1 year later

Notes

Company Name		Ticker Symbol			Industry		Current Market Cap		

Date I First Heard About It	Where I first heard about it			Current Price			52 week high	52 week low	Current Dividend Yield

Under-stand the business	Grow-ing or Stable Industry	Intangible Asset Advantage	Moat	Strong Manage-ment	Insiders Are Buying	Recurring Revenue	Growing Earnings	Healthy Cash Position	Can It Weather a Storm?

PE Ratio	PS Ratio	Projected Rate Growth (5 years)			Price 30 days later	Price 60 days later	Price 90 days later	Price 180 days later	Price 1 year later

Notes

Investing Ideas

Company Name		Ticker Symbol		Industry		Current Market Cap			

Date I First Heard About It	Where I first heard about it			Current Price		52 week high	52 week low	Current Dividend Yield	

Under-stand the business	Grow-ing or Stable Industry	Intangible Asset Advantage	Moat	Strong Manage-ment	Insiders Are Buying	Recurring Revenue	Growing Earnings	Healthy Cash Position	Can It Weather a Storm?

PE Ratio	PS Ratio	Projected Rate Growth (5 years)		Price 30 days later	Price 60 days later	Price 90 days later	Price 180 days later	Price 1 year later	

Notes

Company Name		Ticker Symbol		Industry		Current Market Cap			

Date I First Heard About It	Where I first heard about it			Current Price		52 week high	52 week low	Current Dividend Yield	

Under-stand the business	Grow-ing or Stable Industry	Intangible Asset Advantage	Moat	Strong Manage-ment	Insiders Are Buying	Recurring Revenue	Growing Earnings	Healthy Cash Position	Can It Weather a Storm?

PE Ratio	PS Ratio	Projected Rate Growth (5 years)		Price 30 days later	Price 60 days later	Price 90 days later	Price 180 days later	Price 1 year later	

Notes

Investing Ideas

Company Name		Ticker Symbol		Industry		Current Market Cap			

Date I First Heard About It	Where I first heard about it			Current Price		52 week high	52 week low	Current Dividend Yield	

Under-stand the business	Grow-ing or Stable Industry	Intangible Asset Advantage	Moat	Strong Manage-ment		Insiders Are Buying	Recurring Revenue	Growing Earnings	Healthy Cash Position	Can It Weather a Storm?

PE Ratio	PS Ratio	Projected Rate Growth (5 years)				Price 30 days later	Price 60 days later	Price 90 days later	Price 180 days later	Price 1 year later

Notes

Company Name		Ticker Symbol		Industry		Current Market Cap			

Date I First Heard About It	Where I first heard about it			Current Price		52 week high	52 week low	Current Dividend Yield	

Under-stand the business	Grow-ing or Stable Industry	Intangible Asset Advantage	Moat	Strong Manage-ment		Insiders Are Buying	Recurring Revenue	Growing Earnings	Healthy Cash Position	Can It Weather a Storm?

PE Ratio	PS Ratio	Projected Rate Growth (5 years)				Price 30 days later	Price 60 days later	Price 90 days later	Price 180 days later	Price 1 year later

Notes

Investing Ideas

Company Name		Ticker Symbol		Industry		Current Market Cap		

Date I First Heard About It	Where I first heard about it			Current Price	52 week high	52 week low	Current Dividend Yield

Under-stand the business	Grow-ing or Stable Industry	Intangible Asset Advantage	Moat	Strong Manage-ment	Insiders Are Buying	Recurring Revenue	Growing Earnings	Healthy Cash Position	Can It Weather a Storm?

PE Ratio	PS Ratio	Projected Rate Growth (5 years)		Price 30 days later	Price 60 days later	Price 90 days later	Price 180 days later	Price 1 year later

Notes

Company Name		Ticker Symbol		Industry		Current Market Cap		

Date I First Heard About It	Where I first heard about it			Current Price	52 week high	52 week low	Current Dividend Yield

Under-stand the business	Grow-ing or Stable Industry	Intangible Asset Advantage	Moat	Strong Manage-ment	Insiders Are Buying	Recurring Revenue	Growing Earnings	Healthy Cash Position	Can It Weather a Storm?

PE Ratio	PS Ratio	Projected Rate Growth (5 years)		Price 30 days later	Price 60 days later	Price 90 days later	Price 180 days later	Price 1 year later

Notes

Investing Ideas

Company Name			Ticker Symbol			Industry		Current Market Cap		

Date I First Heard About It	Where I first heard about it			Current Price			52 week high	52 week low	Current Dividend Yield	

Under-stand the business	Grow-ing or Stable Industry	Intangible Asset Advantage	Moat	Strong Manage-ment		Insiders Are Buying	Recurring Revenue	Growing Earnings	Healthy Cash Position	Can It Weather a Storm?

PE Ratio	PS Ratio	Projected Rate Growth (5 years)				Price 30 days later	Price 60 days later	Price 90 days later	Price 180 days later	Price 1 year later

Notes

Company Name			Ticker Symbol			Industry		Current Market Cap		

Date I First Heard About It	Where I first heard about it			Current Price			52 week high	52 week low	Current Dividend Yield	

Under-stand the business	Grow-ing or Stable Industry	Intangible Asset Advantage	Moat	Strong Manage-ment		Insiders Are Buying	Recurring Revenue	Growing Earnings	Healthy Cash Position	Can It Weather a Storm?

PE Ratio	PS Ratio	Projected Rate Growth (5 years)				Price 30 days later	Price 60 days later	Price 90 days later	Price 180 days later	Price 1 year later

Notes

Investing Ideas

Company Name			Ticker Symbol		Industry		Current Market Cap		

Date I First Heard About It	Where I first heard about it			Current Price		52 week high	52 week low	Current Dividend Yield	

Under-stand the business	Grow-ing or Stable Industry	Intangible Asset Advantage	Moat	Strong Manage-ment	Insiders Are Buying	Recurring Revenue	Growing Earnings	Healthy Cash Position	Can It Weather a Storm?

PE Ratio	PS Ratio	Projected Rate Growth (5 years)		Price 30 days later	Price 60 days later	Price 90 days later	Price 180 days later	Price 1 year later

Notes

Company Name			Ticker Symbol		Industry		Current Market Cap		

Date I First Heard About It	Where I first heard about it			Current Price		52 week high	52 week low	Current Dividend Yield	

Under-stand the business	Grow-ing or Stable Industry	Intangible Asset Advantage	Moat	Strong Manage-ment	Insiders Are Buying	Recurring Revenue	Growing Earnings	Healthy Cash Position	Can It Weather a Storm?

PE Ratio	PS Ratio	Projected Rate Growth (5 years)		Price 30 days later	Price 60 days later	Price 90 days later	Price 180 days later	Price 1 year later

Notes

Investing Ideas

Company Name		Ticker Symbol		Industry			Current Market Cap		

Date I First Heard About It	Where I first heard about it			Current Price			52 week high	52 week low	Current Dividend Yield

Under-stand the business	Grow-ing or Stable Industry	Intangible Asset Advantage	Moat	Strong Manage-ment	Insiders Are Buying	Recurring Revenue	Growing Earnings	Healthy Cash Position	Can It Weather a Storm?

PE Ratio	PS Ratio	Projected Rate Growth (5 years)		Price 30 days later	Price 60 days later	Price 90 days later	Price 180 days later	Price 1 year later

Notes

Company Name		Ticker Symbol		Industry			Current Market Cap		

Date I First Heard About It	Where I first heard about it			Current Price			52 week high	52 week low	Current Dividend Yield

Under-stand the business	Grow-ing or Stable Industry	Intangible Asset Advantage	Moat	Strong Manage-ment	Insiders Are Buying	Recurring Revenue	Growing Earnings	Healthy Cash Position	Can It Weather a Storm?

PE Ratio	PS Ratio	Projected Rate Growth (5 years)		Price 30 days later	Price 60 days later	Price 90 days later	Price 180 days later	Price 1 year later

Notes

Investing Ideas

Company Name	Ticker Symbol	Industry	Current Market Cap		

Date I First Heard About It	Where I first heard about it	Current Price	52 week high	52 week low	Current Dividend Yield

Under-stand the business	Grow-ing or Stable Industry	Intangible Asset Advantage	Moat	Strong Manage-ment	Insiders Are Buying	Recurring Revenue	Growing Earnings	Healthy Cash Position	Can It Weather a Storm?

PE Ratio	PS Ratio	Projected Rate Growth (5 years)		Price 30 days later	Price 60 days later	Price 90 days later	Price 180 days later	Price 1 year later

Notes

Company Name	Ticker Symbol	Industry	Current Market Cap		

Date I First Heard About It	Where I first heard about it	Current Price	52 week high	52 week low	Current Dividend Yield

Under-stand the business	Grow-ing or Stable Industry	Intangible Asset Advantage	Moat	Strong Manage-ment	Insiders Are Buying	Recurring Revenue	Growing Earnings	Healthy Cash Position	Can It Weather a Storm?

PE Ratio	PS Ratio	Projected Rate Growth (5 years)		Price 30 days later	Price 60 days later	Price 90 days later	Price 180 days later	Price 1 year later

Notes

Investing Ideas

Company Name			Ticker Symbol			Industry		Current Market Cap		

Date I First Heard About It	Where I first heard about it			Current Price		52 week high	52 week low	Current Dividend Yield

Under-stand the business	Grow-ing or Stable Industry	Intangible Asset Advantage	Moat	Strong Manage-ment	Insiders Are Buying	Recurring Revenue	Growing Earnings	Healthy Cash Position	Can It Weather a Storm?

PE Ratio	PS Ratio	Projected Rate Growth (5 years)		Price 30 days later	Price 60 days later	Price 90 days later	Price 180 days later	Price 1 year later

Notes

Company Name			Ticker Symbol			Industry		Current Market Cap		

Date I First Heard About It	Where I first heard about it			Current Price		52 week high	52 week low	Current Dividend Yield

Under-stand the business	Grow-ing or Stable Industry	Intangible Asset Advantage	Moat	Strong Manage-ment	Insiders Are Buying	Recurring Revenue	Growing Earnings	Healthy Cash Position	Can It Weather a Storm?

PE Ratio	PS Ratio	Projected Rate Growth (5 years)		Price 30 days later	Price 60 days later	Price 90 days later	Price 180 days later	Price 1 year later

Notes

Investing Ideas

Company Name			Ticker Symbol		Industry		Current Market Cap		

Date I First Heard About It	Where I first heard about it			Current Price		52 week high	52 week low	Current Dividend Yield	

Under-stand the business	Grow-ing or Stable Industry	Intangible Asset Advantage	Moat	Strong Manage-ment	Insiders Are Buying	Recurring Revenue	Growing Earnings	Healthy Cash Position	Can It Weather a Storm?

PE Ratio	PS Ratio	Projected Rate Growth (5 years)			Price 30 days later	Price 60 days later	Price 90 days later	Price 180 days later	Price 1 year later

Notes

Company Name			Ticker Symbol		Industry		Current Market Cap		

Date I First Heard About It	Where I first heard about it			Current Price		52 week high	52 week low	Current Dividend Yield	

Under-stand the business	Grow-ing or Stable Industry	Intangible Asset Advantage	Moat	Strong Manage-ment	Insiders Are Buying	Recurring Revenue	Growing Earnings	Healthy Cash Position	Can It Weather a Storm?

PE Ratio	PS Ratio	Projected Rate Growth (5 years)			Price 30 days later	Price 60 days later	Price 90 days later	Price 180 days later	Price 1 year later

Notes

Investing Ideas

Company Name		Ticker Symbol		Industry		Current Market Cap		

Date I First Heard About It	Where I first heard about it			Current Price	52 week high	52 week low	Current Dividend Yield

Under-stand the business	Grow-ing or Stable Industry	Intangible Asset Advantage	Moat	Strong Manage-ment	Insiders Are Buying	Recurring Revenue	Growing Earnings	Healthy Cash Position	Can It Weather a Storm?

PE Ratio	PS Ratio	Projected Rate Growth (5 years)		Price 30 days later	Price 60 days later	Price 90 days later	Price 180 days later	Price 1 year later

Notes

Company Name		Ticker Symbol		Industry		Current Market Cap		

Date I First Heard About It	Where I first heard about it			Current Price	52 week high	52 week low	Current Dividend Yield

Under-stand the business	Grow-ing or Stable Industry	Intangible Asset Advantage	Moat	Strong Manage-ment	Insiders Are Buying	Recurring Revenue	Growing Earnings	Healthy Cash Position	Can It Weather a Storm?

PE Ratio	PS Ratio	Projected Rate Growth (5 years)		Price 30 days later	Price 60 days later	Price 90 days later	Price 180 days later	Price 1 year later

Notes

Investing Ideas

Company Name			Ticker Symbol		Industry		Current Market Cap		

Date I First Heard About It	Where I first heard about it				Current Price		52 week high	52 week low	Current Dividend Yield

Under-stand the business	Grow-ing or Stable Industry	Intangible Asset Advantage	Moat	Strong Manage-ment	Insiders Are Buying	Recurring Revenue	Growing Earnings	Healthy Cash Position	Can It Weather a Storm?

PE Ratio	PS Ratio	Projected Rate Growth (5 years)			Price 30 days later	Price 60 days later	Price 90 days later	Price 180 days later	Price 1 year later

Notes

Company Name			Ticker Symbol		Industry		Current Market Cap		

Date I First Heard About It	Where I first heard about it				Current Price		52 week high	52 week low	Current Dividend Yield

Under-stand the business	Grow-ing or Stable Industry	Intangible Asset Advantage	Moat	Strong Manage-ment	Insiders Are Buying	Recurring Revenue	Growing Earnings	Healthy Cash Position	Can It Weather a Storm?

PE Ratio	PS Ratio	Projected Rate Growth (5 years)			Price 30 days later	Price 60 days later	Price 90 days later	Price 180 days later	Price 1 year later

Notes

Investing Ideas

Company Name		Ticker Symbol		Industry		Current Market Cap		

Date I First Heard About It	Where I first heard about it			Current Price	52 week high	52 week low	Current Dividend Yield

Under-stand the business	Grow-ing or Stable Industry	Intangible Asset Advantage	Moat	Strong Manage-ment	Insiders Are Buying	Recurring Revenue	Growing Earnings	Healthy Cash Position	Can It Weather a Storm?

PE Ratio	PS Ratio	Projected Rate Growth (5 years)		Price 30 days later	Price 60 days later	Price 90 days later	Price 180 days later	Price 1 year later

Notes

Company Name		Ticker Symbol		Industry		Current Market Cap		

Date I First Heard About It	Where I first heard about it			Current Price	52 week high	52 week low	Current Dividend Yield

Under-stand the business	Grow-ing or Stable Industry	Intangible Asset Advantage	Moat	Strong Manage-ment	Insiders Are Buying	Recurring Revenue	Growing Earnings	Healthy Cash Position	Can It Weather a Storm?

PE Ratio	PS Ratio	Projected Rate Growth (5 years)		Price 30 days later	Price 60 days later	Price 90 days later	Price 180 days later	Price 1 year later

Notes

Investing Ideas

Company Name		Ticker Symbol		Industry			Current Market Cap		

Date I First Heard About It	Where I first heard about it			Current Price			52 week high	52 week low	Current Dividend Yield

Under-stand the business	Grow-ing or Stable Industry	Intangible Asset Advantage	Moat	Strong Manage-ment	Insiders Are Buying	Recurring Revenue	Growing Earnings	Healthy Cash Position	Can It Weather a Storm?

PE Ratio	PS Ratio	Projected Rate Growth (5 years)		Price 30 days later	Price 60 days later	Price 90 days later	Price 180 days later	Price 1 year later

Notes

Company Name		Ticker Symbol		Industry			Current Market Cap		

Date I First Heard About It	Where I first heard about it			Current Price			52 week high	52 week low	Current Dividend Yield

Under-stand the business	Grow-ing or Stable Industry	Intangible Asset Advantage	Moat	Strong Manage-ment	Insiders Are Buying	Recurring Revenue	Growing Earnings	Healthy Cash Position	Can It Weather a Storm?

PE Ratio	PS Ratio	Projected Rate Growth (5 years)		Price 30 days later	Price 60 days later	Price 90 days later	Price 180 days later	Price 1 year later

Notes

Investing Ideas

Company Name		Ticker Symbol		Industry		Current Market Cap			

Date I First Heard About It	Where I first heard about it			Current Price		52 week high	52 week low	Current Dividend Yield	

Under-stand the business	Grow-ing or Stable Industry	Intangible Asset Advantage	Moat	Strong Manage-ment	Insiders Are Buying	Recurring Revenue	Growing Earnings	Healthy Cash Position	Can It Weather a Storm?

PE Ratio	PS Ratio	Projected Rate Growth (5 years)		Price 30 days later	Price 60 days later	Price 90 days later	Price 180 days later	Price 1 year later	

Notes

Company Name		Ticker Symbol		Industry		Current Market Cap			

Date I First Heard About It	Where I first heard about it			Current Price		52 week high	52 week low	Current Dividend Yield	

Under-stand the business	Grow-ing or Stable Industry	Intangible Asset Advantage	Moat	Strong Manage-ment	Insiders Are Buying	Recurring Revenue	Growing Earnings	Healthy Cash Position	Can It Weather a Storm?

PE Ratio	PS Ratio	Projected Rate Growth (5 years)		Price 30 days later	Price 60 days later	Price 90 days later	Price 180 days later	Price 1 year later	

Notes

Investing Ideas

Company Name		Ticker Symbol		Industry		Current Market Cap		

Date I First Heard About It	Where I first heard about it			Current Price	52 week high	52 week low	Current Dividend Yield

Under-stand the business	Grow-ing or Stable Industry	Intangible Asset Advantage	Moat	Strong Manage-ment	Insiders Are Buying	Recurring Revenue	Growing Earnings	Healthy Cash Position	Can It Weather a Storm?

PE Ratio	PS Ratio	Projected Rate Growth (5 years)		Price 30 days later	Price 60 days later	Price 90 days later	Price 180 days later	Price 1 year later

Notes

Company Name		Ticker Symbol		Industry		Current Market Cap		

Date I First Heard About It	Where I first heard about it			Current Price	52 week high	52 week low	Current Dividend Yield

Under-stand the business	Grow-ing or Stable Industry	Intangible Asset Advantage	Moat	Strong Manage-ment	Insiders Are Buying	Recurring Revenue	Growing Earnings	Healthy Cash Position	Can It Weather a Storm?

PE Ratio	PS Ratio	Projected Rate Growth (5 years)		Price 30 days later	Price 60 days later	Price 90 days later	Price 180 days later	Price 1 year later

Notes

Investing Ideas

Company Name			Ticker Symbol			Industry		Current Market Cap		

Date I First Heard About It	Where I first heard about it			Current Price		52 week high	52 week low	Current Dividend Yield

Under-stand the business	Grow-ing or Stable Industry	Intangible Asset Advantage	Moat	Strong Manage-ment	Insiders Are Buying	Recurring Revenue	Growing Earnings	Healthy Cash Position	Can It Weather a Storm?

PE Ratio	PS Ratio	Projected Rate Growth (5 years)		Price 30 days later	Price 60 days later	Price 90 days later	Price 180 days later	Price 1 year later

Notes

Company Name			Ticker Symbol			Industry		Current Market Cap		

Date I First Heard About It	Where I first heard about it			Current Price		52 week high	52 week low	Current Dividend Yield

Under-stand the business	Grow-ing or Stable Industry	Intangible Asset Advantage	Moat	Strong Manage-ment	Insiders Are Buying	Recurring Revenue	Growing Earnings	Healthy Cash Position	Can It Weather a Storm?

PE Ratio	PS Ratio	Projected Rate Growth (5 years)		Price 30 days later	Price 60 days later	Price 90 days later	Price 180 days later	Price 1 year later

Notes

Investing Ideas

Company Name		Ticker Symbol		Industry		Current Market Cap		

Date I First Heard About It	Where I first heard about it			Current Price	52 week high	52 week low	Current Dividend Yield

Under-stand the business	Grow-ing or Stable Industry	Intangible Asset Advantage	Moat	Strong Manage-ment	Insiders Are Buying	Recurring Revenue	Growing Earnings	Healthy Cash Position	Can It Weather a Storm?

PE Ratio	PS Ratio	Projected Rate Growth (5 years)		Price 30 days later	Price 60 days later	Price 90 days later	Price 180 days later	Price 1 year later

Notes

Company Name		Ticker Symbol		Industry		Current Market Cap		

Date I First Heard About It	Where I first heard about it			Current Price	52 week high	52 week low	Current Dividend Yield

Under-stand the business	Grow-ing or Stable Industry	Intangible Asset Advantage	Moat	Strong Manage-ment	Insiders Are Buying	Recurring Revenue	Growing Earnings	Healthy Cash Position	Can It Weather a Storm?

PE Ratio	PS Ratio	Projected Rate Growth (5 years)		Price 30 days later	Price 60 days later	Price 90 days later	Price 180 days later	Price 1 year later

Notes

Investing Ideas

Company Name		Ticker Symbol		Industry			Current Market Cap		

Date I First Heard About It	Where I first heard about it			Current Price		52 week high	52 week low	Current Dividend Yield	

Under-stand the business	Grow-ing or Stable Industry	Intangible Asset Advantage	Moat	Strong Manage-ment		Insiders Are Buying	Recurring Revenue	Growing Earnings	Healthy Cash Position	Can It Weather a Storm?

PE Ratio	PS Ratio	Projected Rate Growth (5 years)				Price 30 days later	Price 60 days later	Price 90 days later	Price 180 days later	Price 1 year later

Notes

Company Name		Ticker Symbol		Industry			Current Market Cap		

Date I First Heard About It	Where I first heard about it			Current Price		52 week high	52 week low	Current Dividend Yield	

Under-stand the business	Grow-ing or Stable Industry	Intangible Asset Advantage	Moat	Strong Manage-ment		Insiders Are Buying	Recurring Revenue	Growing Earnings	Healthy Cash Position	Can It Weather a Storm?

PE Ratio	PS Ratio	Projected Rate Growth (5 years)				Price 30 days later	Price 60 days later	Price 90 days later	Price 180 days later	Price 1 year later

Notes

Investing Ideas

Company Name		Ticker Symbol		Industry		Current Market Cap		

Date I First Heard About It	Where I first heard about it			Current Price	52 week high	52 week low	Current Dividend Yield

Under-stand the business	Grow-ing or Stable Industry	Intangible Asset Advantage	Moat	Strong Manage-ment	Insiders Are Buying	Recurring Revenue	Growing Earnings	Healthy Cash Position	Can It Weather a Storm?

PE Ratio	PS Ratio	Projected Rate Growth (5 years)			Price 30 days later	Price 60 days later	Price 90 days later	Price 180 days later	Price 1 year later

Notes

Company Name		Ticker Symbol		Industry		Current Market Cap		

Date I First Heard About It	Where I first heard about it			Current Price	52 week high	52 week low	Current Dividend Yield

Under-stand the business	Grow-ing or Stable Industry	Intangible Asset Advantage	Moat	Strong Manage-ment	Insiders Are Buying	Recurring Revenue	Growing Earnings	Healthy Cash Position	Can It Weather a Storm?

PE Ratio	PS Ratio	Projected Rate Growth (5 years)			Price 30 days later	Price 60 days later	Price 90 days later	Price 180 days later	Price 1 year later

Notes

Investing Ideas

Company Name			Ticker Symbol			Industry		Current Market Cap		

Date I First Heard About It	Where I first heard about it			Current Price		52 week high	52 week low	Current Dividend Yield

Under-stand the business	Grow-ing or Stable Industry	Intangible Asset Advantage	Moat	Strong Manage-ment	Insiders Are Buying	Recurring Revenue	Growing Earnings	Healthy Cash Position	Can It Weather a Storm?

PE Ratio	PS Ratio	Projected Rate Growth (5 years)		Price 30 days later	Price 60 days later	Price 90 days later	Price 180 days later	Price 1 year later

Notes

Company Name			Ticker Symbol			Industry		Current Market Cap		

Date I First Heard About It	Where I first heard about it			Current Price		52 week high	52 week low	Current Dividend Yield

Under-stand the business	Grow-ing or Stable Industry	Intangible Asset Advantage	Moat	Strong Manage-ment	Insiders Are Buying	Recurring Revenue	Growing Earnings	Healthy Cash Position	Can It Weather a Storm?

PE Ratio	PS Ratio	Projected Rate Growth (5 years)		Price 30 days later	Price 60 days later	Price 90 days later	Price 180 days later	Price 1 year later

Notes

Investing Ideas

Company Name			Ticker Symbol		Industry		Current Market Cap		

Date I First Heard About It	Where I first heard about it				Current Price		52 week high	52 week low	Current Dividend Yield

Understand the business	Growing or Stable Industry	Intangible Asset Advantage	Moat	Strong Management	Insiders Are Buying	Recurring Revenue	Growing Earnings	Healthy Cash Position	Can It Weather a Storm?

PE Ratio	PS Ratio	Projected Rate Growth (5 years)			Price 30 days later	Price 60 days later	Price 90 days later	Price 180 days later	Price 1 year later

Notes

Company Name			Ticker Symbol		Industry		Current Market Cap		

Date I First Heard About It	Where I first heard about it				Current Price		52 week high	52 week low	Current Dividend Yield

Understand the business	Growing or Stable Industry	Intangible Asset Advantage	Moat	Strong Management	Insiders Are Buying	Recurring Revenue	Growing Earnings	Healthy Cash Position	Can It Weather a Storm?

PE Ratio	PS Ratio	Projected Rate Growth (5 years)			Price 30 days later	Price 60 days later	Price 90 days later	Price 180 days later	Price 1 year later

Notes

Investing Ideas

Company Name			Ticker Symbol		Industry		Current Market Cap			

Date I First Heard About It	Where I first heard about it			Current Price		52 week high	52 week low	Current Dividend Yield

Under-stand the business	Grow-ing or Stable Industry	Intangible Asset Advantage	Moat	Strong Manage-ment	Insiders Are Buying	Recurring Revenue	Growing Earnings	Healthy Cash Position	Can It Weather a Storm?

PE Ratio	PS Ratio	Projected Rate Growth (5 years)		Price 30 days later	Price 60 days later	Price 90 days later	Price 180 days later	Price 1 year later

Notes

Company Name			Ticker Symbol		Industry		Current Market Cap			

Date I First Heard About It	Where I first heard about it			Current Price		52 week high	52 week low	Current Dividend Yield

Under-stand the business	Grow-ing or Stable Industry	Intangible Asset Advantage	Moat	Strong Manage-ment	Insiders Are Buying	Recurring Revenue	Growing Earnings	Healthy Cash Position	Can It Weather a Storm?

PE Ratio	PS Ratio	Projected Rate Growth (5 years)		Price 30 days later	Price 60 days later	Price 90 days later	Price 180 days later	Price 1 year later

Notes

Investing Ideas

Company Name			Ticker Symbol		Industry		Current Market Cap		

Date I First Heard About It	Where I first heard about it			Current Price			52 week high	52 week low	Current Dividend Yield

Under-stand the business	Grow-ing or Stable Industry	Intangible Asset Advantage	Moat	Strong Manage-ment	Insiders Are Buying	Recurring Revenue	Growing Earnings	Healthy Cash Position	Can It Weather a Storm?

PE Ratio	PS Ratio	Projected Rate Growth (5 years)			Price 30 days later	Price 60 days later	Price 90 days later	Price 180 days later	Price 1 year later

Notes

Company Name			Ticker Symbol		Industry		Current Market Cap		

Date I First Heard About It	Where I first heard about it			Current Price			52 week high	52 week low	Current Dividend Yield

Under-stand the business	Grow-ing or Stable Industry	Intangible Asset Advantage	Moat	Strong Manage-ment	Insiders Are Buying	Recurring Revenue	Growing Earnings	Healthy Cash Position	Can It Weather a Storm?

PE Ratio	PS Ratio	Projected Rate Growth (5 years)			Price 30 days later	Price 60 days later	Price 90 days later	Price 180 days later	Price 1 year later

Notes

Investing Ideas

Company Name			Ticker Symbol			Industry		Current Market Cap		

Date I First Heard About It	Where I first heard about it			Current Price		52 week high	52 week low	Current Dividend Yield

Under-stand the business	Grow-ing or Stable Industry	Intangible Asset Advantage	Moat	Strong Manage-ment	Insiders Are Buying	Recurring Revenue	Growing Earnings	Healthy Cash Position	Can It Weather a Storm?

PE Ratio	PS Ratio	Projected Rate Growth (5 years)		Price 30 days later	Price 60 days later	Price 90 days later	Price 180 days later	Price 1 year later

Notes

Company Name			Ticker Symbol			Industry		Current Market Cap		

Date I First Heard About It	Where I first heard about it			Current Price		52 week high	52 week low	Current Dividend Yield

Under-stand the business	Grow-ing or Stable Industry	Intangible Asset Advantage	Moat	Strong Manage-ment	Insiders Are Buying	Recurring Revenue	Growing Earnings	Healthy Cash Position	Can It Weather a Storm?

PE Ratio	PS Ratio	Projected Rate Growth (5 years)		Price 30 days later	Price 60 days later	Price 90 days later	Price 180 days later	Price 1 year later

Notes

Investing Ideas

Company Name		Ticker Symbol		Industry		Current Market Cap		

Date I First Heard About It	Where I first heard about it			Current Price	52 week high	52 week low	Current Dividend Yield

Under-stand the business	Grow-ing or Stable Industry	Intangible Asset Advantage	Moat	Strong Manage-ment	Insiders Are Buying	Recurring Revenue	Growing Earnings	Healthy Cash Position	Can It Weather a Storm?

PE Ratio	PS Ratio	Projected Rate Growth (5 years)			Price 30 days later	Price 60 days later	Price 90 days later	Price 180 days later	Price 1 year later

Notes

Company Name		Ticker Symbol		Industry		Current Market Cap		

Date I First Heard About It	Where I first heard about it			Current Price	52 week high	52 week low	Current Dividend Yield

Under-stand the business	Grow-ing or Stable Industry	Intangible Asset Advantage	Moat	Strong Manage-ment	Insiders Are Buying	Recurring Revenue	Growing Earnings	Healthy Cash Position	Can It Weather a Storm?

PE Ratio	PS Ratio	Projected Rate Growth (5 years)			Price 30 days later	Price 60 days later	Price 90 days later	Price 180 days later	Price 1 year later

Notes

Investing Ideas

Company Name		Ticker Symbol		Industry		Current Market Cap		

Date I First Heard About It	Where I first heard about it			Current Price		52 week high	52 week low	Current Dividend Yield

Under-stand the business	Grow-ing or Stable Industry	Intangible Asset Advantage	Moat	Strong Manage-ment	Insiders Are Buying	Recurring Revenue	Growing Earnings	Healthy Cash Position	Can It Weather a Storm?

PE Ratio	PS Ratio	Projected Rate Growth (5 years)		Price 30 days later	Price 60 days later	Price 90 days later	Price 180 days later	Price 1 year later

Notes

Company Name		Ticker Symbol		Industry		Current Market Cap		

Date I First Heard About It	Where I first heard about it			Current Price		52 week high	52 week low	Current Dividend Yield

Under-stand the business	Grow-ing or Stable Industry	Intangible Asset Advantage	Moat	Strong Manage-ment	Insiders Are Buying	Recurring Revenue	Growing Earnings	Healthy Cash Position	Can It Weather a Storm?

PE Ratio	PS Ratio	Projected Rate Growth (5 years)		Price 30 days later	Price 60 days later	Price 90 days later	Price 180 days later	Price 1 year later

Notes

Investing Ideas

Company Name		Ticker Symbol		Industry		Current Market Cap		

Date I First Heard About It	Where I first heard about it			Current Price	52 week high	52 week low	Current Dividend Yield

Under-stand the business	Grow-ing or Stable Industry	Intangible Asset Advantage	Moat	Strong Manage-ment	Insiders Are Buying	Recurring Revenue	Growing Earnings	Healthy Cash Position	Can It Weather a Storm?

PE Ratio	PS Ratio	Projected Rate Growth (5 years)		Price 30 days later	Price 60 days later	Price 90 days later	Price 180 days later	Price 1 year later

Notes

Company Name		Ticker Symbol		Industry		Current Market Cap		

Date I First Heard About It	Where I first heard about it			Current Price	52 week high	52 week low	Current Dividend Yield

Under-stand the business	Grow-ing or Stable Industry	Intangible Asset Advantage	Moat	Strong Manage-ment	Insiders Are Buying	Recurring Revenue	Growing Earnings	Healthy Cash Position	Can It Weather a Storm?

PE Ratio	PS Ratio	Projected Rate Growth (5 years)		Price 30 days later	Price 60 days later	Price 90 days later	Price 180 days later	Price 1 year later

Notes

Investing Ideas

Company Name			Ticker Symbol			Industry		Current Market Cap		

Date I First Heard About It	Where I first heard about it			Current Price		52 week high	52 week low	Current Dividend Yield

Under-stand the business	Grow-ing or Stable Industry	Intangible Asset Advantage	Moat	Strong Manage-ment	Insiders Are Buying	Recurring Revenue	Growing Earnings	Healthy Cash Position	Can It Weather a Storm?

PE Ratio	PS Ratio	Projected Rate Growth (5 years)		Price 30 days later	Price 60 days later	Price 90 days later	Price 180 days later	Price 1 year later

Notes

Company Name			Ticker Symbol			Industry		Current Market Cap		

Date I First Heard About It	Where I first heard about it			Current Price		52 week high	52 week low	Current Dividend Yield

Under-stand the business	Grow-ing or Stable Industry	Intangible Asset Advantage	Moat	Strong Manage-ment	Insiders Are Buying	Recurring Revenue	Growing Earnings	Healthy Cash Position	Can It Weather a Storm?

PE Ratio	PS Ratio	Projected Rate Growth (5 years)		Price 30 days later	Price 60 days later	Price 90 days later	Price 180 days later	Price 1 year later

Notes

Investing Ideas

Company Name	Ticker Symbol	Industry	Current Market Cap		

Date I First Heard About It	Where I first heard about it		Current Price	52 week high	52 week low	Current Dividend Yield

Under-stand the business	Grow-ing or Stable Industry	Intangible Asset Advantage	Moat	Strong Manage-ment	Insiders Are Buying	Recurring Revenue	Growing Earnings	Healthy Cash Position	Can It Weather a Storm?

PE Ratio	PS Ratio	Projected Rate Growth (5 years)		Price 30 days later	Price 60 days later	Price 90 days later	Price 180 days later	Price 1 year later

Notes

Company Name	Ticker Symbol	Industry	Current Market Cap		

Date I First Heard About It	Where I first heard about it		Current Price	52 week high	52 week low	Current Dividend Yield

Under-stand the business	Grow-ing or Stable Industry	Intangible Asset Advantage	Moat	Strong Manage-ment	Insiders Are Buying	Recurring Revenue	Growing Earnings	Healthy Cash Position	Can It Weather a Storm?

PE Ratio	PS Ratio	Projected Rate Growth (5 years)		Price 30 days later	Price 60 days later	Price 90 days later	Price 180 days later	Price 1 year later

Notes

Investing Ideas

Company Name		Ticker Symbol		Industry		Current Market Cap			

Date I First Heard About It	Where I first heard about it			Current Price		52 week high	52 week low	Current Dividend Yield	

Under-stand the business	Grow-ing or Stable Industry	Intangible Asset Advantage	Moat	Strong Manage-ment	Insiders Are Buying	Recurring Revenue	Growing Earnings	Healthy Cash Position	Can It Weather a Storm?

PE Ratio	PS Ratio	Projected Rate Growth (5 years)			Price 30 days later	Price 60 days later	Price 90 days later	Price 180 days later	Price 1 year later

Notes

Company Name		Ticker Symbol		Industry		Current Market Cap			

Date I First Heard About It	Where I first heard about it			Current Price		52 week high	52 week low	Current Dividend Yield	

Under-stand the business	Grow-ing or Stable Industry	Intangible Asset Advantage	Moat	Strong Manage-ment	Insiders Are Buying	Recurring Revenue	Growing Earnings	Healthy Cash Position	Can It Weather a Storm?

PE Ratio	PS Ratio	Projected Rate Growth (5 years)			Price 30 days later	Price 60 days later	Price 90 days later	Price 180 days later	Price 1 year later

Notes

Investing Ideas

Company Name		Ticker Symbol		Industry			Current Market Cap		

Date I First Heard About It	Where I first heard about it			Current Price		52 week high	52 week low	Current Dividend Yield

Under-stand the business	Grow-ing or Stable Industry	Intangible Asset Advantage	Moat	Strong Manage-ment	Insiders Are Buying	Recurring Revenue	Growing Earnings	Healthy Cash Position	Can It Weather a Storm?

PE Ratio	PS Ratio	Projected Rate Growth (5 years)		Price 30 days later	Price 60 days later	Price 90 days later	Price 180 days later	Price 1 year later

Notes

Company Name		Ticker Symbol		Industry			Current Market Cap		

Date I First Heard About It	Where I first heard about it			Current Price		52 week high	52 week low	Current Dividend Yield

Under-stand the business	Grow-ing or Stable Industry	Intangible Asset Advantage	Moat	Strong Manage-ment	Insiders Are Buying	Recurring Revenue	Growing Earnings	Healthy Cash Position	Can It Weather a Storm?

PE Ratio	PS Ratio	Projected Rate Growth (5 years)		Price 30 days later	Price 60 days later	Price 90 days later	Price 180 days later	Price 1 year later

Notes

Investing Ideas

Company Name			Ticker Symbol			Industry		Current Market Cap		

Date I First Heard About It	Where I first heard about it			Current Price		52 week high	52 week low	Current Dividend Yield

Under-stand the business	Grow-ing or Stable Industry	Intangible Asset Advantage	Moat	Strong Manage-ment	Insiders Are Buying	Recurring Revenue	Growing Earnings	Healthy Cash Position	Can It Weather a Storm?

PE Ratio	PS Ratio	Projected Rate Growth (5 years)			Price 30 days later	Price 60 days later	Price 90 days later	Price 180 days later	Price 1 year later

Notes

Company Name			Ticker Symbol			Industry		Current Market Cap		

Date I First Heard About It	Where I first heard about it			Current Price		52 week high	52 week low	Current Dividend Yield

Under-stand the business	Grow-ing or Stable Industry	Intangible Asset Advantage	Moat	Strong Manage-ment	Insiders Are Buying	Recurring Revenue	Growing Earnings	Healthy Cash Position	Can It Weather a Storm?

PE Ratio	PS Ratio	Projected Rate Growth (5 years)			Price 30 days later	Price 60 days later	Price 90 days later	Price 180 days later	Price 1 year later

Notes

Investing Ideas

Company Name		Ticker Symbol		Industry			Current Market Cap		

Date I First Heard About It	Where I first heard about it			Current Price			52 week high	52 week low	Current Dividend Yield

Under-stand the business	Grow-ing or Stable Industry	Intangible Asset Advantage	Moat	Strong Manage-ment	Insiders Are Buying	Recurring Revenue	Growing Earnings	Healthy Cash Position	Can It Weather a Storm?

PE Ratio	PS Ratio	Projected Rate Growth (5 years)		Price 30 days later	Price 60 days later	Price 90 days later	Price 180 days later	Price 1 year later

Notes

Company Name		Ticker Symbol		Industry			Current Market Cap		

Date I First Heard About It	Where I first heard about it			Current Price			52 week high	52 week low	Current Dividend Yield

Under-stand the business	Grow-ing or Stable Industry	Intangible Asset Advantage	Moat	Strong Manage-ment	Insiders Are Buying	Recurring Revenue	Growing Earnings	Healthy Cash Position	Can It Weather a Storm?

PE Ratio	PS Ratio	Projected Rate Growth (5 years)		Price 30 days later	Price 60 days later	Price 90 days later	Price 180 days later	Price 1 year later

Notes

Investing Ideas

Company Name		Ticker Symbol			Industry		Current Market Cap		

Date I First Heard About It	Where I first heard about it				Current Price		52 week high	52 week low	Current Dividend Yield

Understand the business	Growing or Stable Industry	Intangible Asset Advantage	Moat	Strong Management	Insiders Are Buying	Recurring Revenue	Growing Earnings	Healthy Cash Position	Can It Weather a Storm?

PE Ratio	PS Ratio	Projected Rate Growth (5 years)			Price 30 days later	Price 60 days later	Price 90 days later	Price 180 days later	Price 1 year later

Notes

Company Name		Ticker Symbol			Industry		Current Market Cap		

Date I First Heard About It	Where I first heard about it				Current Price		52 week high	52 week low	Current Dividend Yield

Understand the business	Growing or Stable Industry	Intangible Asset Advantage	Moat	Strong Management	Insiders Are Buying	Recurring Revenue	Growing Earnings	Healthy Cash Position	Can It Weather a Storm?

PE Ratio	PS Ratio	Projected Rate Growth (5 years)			Price 30 days later	Price 60 days later	Price 90 days later	Price 180 days later	Price 1 year later

Notes

Investing Ideas

Company Name		Ticker Symbol		Industry		Current Market Cap		

Date I First Heard About It	Where I first heard about it			Current Price	52 week high	52 week low	Current Dividend Yield

Under-stand the business	Grow-ing or Stable Industry	Intangible Asset Advantage	Moat	Strong Manage-ment	Insiders Are Buying	Recurring Revenue	Growing Earnings	Healthy Cash Position	Can It Weather a Storm?

PE Ratio	PS Ratio	Projected Rate Growth (5 years)		Price 30 days later	Price 60 days later	Price 90 days later	Price 180 days later	Price 1 year later

Notes

Company Name		Ticker Symbol		Industry		Current Market Cap		

Date I First Heard About It	Where I first heard about it			Current Price	52 week high	52 week low	Current Dividend Yield

Under-stand the business	Grow-ing or Stable Industry	Intangible Asset Advantage	Moat	Strong Manage-ment	Insiders Are Buying	Recurring Revenue	Growing Earnings	Healthy Cash Position	Can It Weather a Storm?

PE Ratio	PS Ratio	Projected Rate Growth (5 years)		Price 30 days later	Price 60 days later	Price 90 days later	Price 180 days later	Price 1 year later

Notes

Investing Ideas

Company Name		Ticker Symbol		Industry		Current Market Cap			

Date I First Heard About It	Where I first heard about it			Current Price		52 week high	52 week low	Current Dividend Yield

Under-stand the business	Grow-ing or Stable Industry	Intangible Asset Advantage	Moat	Strong Manage-ment	Insiders Are Buying	Recurring Revenue	Growing Earnings	Healthy Cash Position	Can It Weather a Storm?

PE Ratio	PS Ratio	Projected Rate Growth (5 years)		Price 30 days later	Price 60 days later	Price 90 days later	Price 180 days later	Price 1 year later

Notes

Company Name		Ticker Symbol		Industry		Current Market Cap			

Date I First Heard About It	Where I first heard about it			Current Price		52 week high	52 week low	Current Dividend Yield

Under-stand the business	Grow-ing or Stable Industry	Intangible Asset Advantage	Moat	Strong Manage-ment	Insiders Are Buying	Recurring Revenue	Growing Earnings	Healthy Cash Position	Can It Weather a Storm?

PE Ratio	PS Ratio	Projected Rate Growth (5 years)		Price 30 days later	Price 60 days later	Price 90 days later	Price 180 days later	Price 1 year later

Notes

Investing Ideas

Company Name			Ticker Symbol		Industry		Current Market Cap		

Date I First Heard About It	Where I first heard about it			Current Price		52 week high	52 week low	Current Dividend Yield

Under-stand the business	Grow-ing or Stable Industry	Intangible Asset Advantage	Moat	Strong Manage-ment	Insiders Are Buying	Recurring Revenue	Growing Earnings	Healthy Cash Position	Can It Weather a Storm?

PE Ratio	PS Ratio	Projected Rate Growth (5 years)		Price 30 days later	Price 60 days later	Price 90 days later	Price 180 days later	Price 1 year later

Notes

Company Name			Ticker Symbol		Industry		Current Market Cap		

Date I First Heard About It	Where I first heard about it			Current Price		52 week high	52 week low	Current Dividend Yield

Under-stand the business	Grow-ing or Stable Industry	Intangible Asset Advantage	Moat	Strong Manage-ment	Insiders Are Buying	Recurring Revenue	Growing Earnings	Healthy Cash Position	Can It Weather a Storm?

PE Ratio	PS Ratio	Projected Rate Growth (5 years)		Price 30 days later	Price 60 days later	Price 90 days later	Price 180 days later	Price 1 year later

Notes

Investing Ideas

Company Name			Ticker Symbol			Industry		Current Market Cap		

Date I First Heard About It	Where I first heard about it			Current Price		52 week high	52 week low	Current Dividend Yield

Under-stand the business	Grow-ing or Stable Industry	Intangible Asset Advantage	Moat	Strong Manage-ment	Insiders Are Buying	Recurring Revenue	Growing Earnings	Healthy Cash Position	Can It Weather a Storm?

PE Ratio	PS Ratio	Projected Rate Growth (5 years)		Price 30 days later	Price 60 days later	Price 90 days later	Price 180 days later	Price 1 year later

Notes

Company Name			Ticker Symbol			Industry		Current Market Cap		

Date I First Heard About It	Where I first heard about it			Current Price		52 week high	52 week low	Current Dividend Yield

Under-stand the business	Grow-ing or Stable Industry	Intangible Asset Advantage	Moat	Strong Manage-ment	Insiders Are Buying	Recurring Revenue	Growing Earnings	Healthy Cash Position	Can It Weather a Storm?

PE Ratio	PS Ratio	Projected Rate Growth (5 years)		Price 30 days later	Price 60 days later	Price 90 days later	Price 180 days later	Price 1 year later

Notes

Investing Ideas

Company Name		Ticker Symbol			Industry		Current Market Cap		

Date I First Heard About It	Where I first heard about it				Current Price	52 week high	52 week low	Current Dividend Yield

Under-stand the business	Grow-ing or Stable Industry	Intangible Asset Advantage	Moat	Strong Manage-ment	Insiders Are Buying	Recurring Revenue	Growing Earnings	Healthy Cash Position	Can It Weather a Storm?

PE Ratio	PS Ratio	Projected Rate Growth (5 years)			Price 30 days later	Price 60 days later	Price 90 days later	Price 180 days later	Price 1 year later

Notes

Company Name		Ticker Symbol			Industry		Current Market Cap		

Date I First Heard About It	Where I first heard about it				Current Price	52 week high	52 week low	Current Dividend Yield

Under-stand the business	Grow-ing or Stable Industry	Intangible Asset Advantage	Moat	Strong Manage-ment	Insiders Are Buying	Recurring Revenue	Growing Earnings	Healthy Cash Position	Can It Weather a Storm?

PE Ratio	PS Ratio	Projected Rate Growth (5 years)			Price 30 days later	Price 60 days later	Price 90 days later	Price 180 days later	Price 1 year later

Notes

Investing Ideas

Company Name			Ticker Symbol			Industry		Current Market Cap		

Date I First Heard About It	Where I first heard about it			Current Price		52 week high	52 week low	Current Dividend Yield

Under-stand the business	Grow-ing or Stable Industry	Intangible Asset Advantage	Moat	Strong Manage-ment	Insiders Are Buying	Recurring Revenue	Growing Earnings	Healthy Cash Position	Can It Weather a Storm?

PE Ratio	PS Ratio	Projected Rate Growth (5 years)		Price 30 days later	Price 60 days later	Price 90 days later	Price 180 days later	Price 1 year later

Notes

Company Name			Ticker Symbol			Industry		Current Market Cap		

Date I First Heard About It	Where I first heard about it			Current Price		52 week high	52 week low	Current Dividend Yield

Under-stand the business	Grow-ing or Stable Industry	Intangible Asset Advantage	Moat	Strong Manage-ment	Insiders Are Buying	Recurring Revenue	Growing Earnings	Healthy Cash Position	Can It Weather a Storm?

PE Ratio	PS Ratio	Projected Rate Growth (5 years)		Price 30 days later	Price 60 days later	Price 90 days later	Price 180 days later	Price 1 year later

Notes

Investing Ideas

Company Name	Ticker Symbol	Industry	Current Market Cap		

Date I First Heard About It	Where I first heard about it	Current Price	52 week high	52 week low	Current Dividend Yield

Under-stand the business	Grow-ing or Stable Industry	Intangible Asset Advantage	Moat	Strong Manage-ment	Insiders Are Buying	Recurring Revenue	Growing Earnings	Healthy Cash Position	Can It Weather a Storm?

PE Ratio	PS Ratio	Projected Rate Growth (5 years)			Price 30 days later	Price 60 days later	Price 90 days later	Price 180 days later	Price 1 year later

Notes

Company Name	Ticker Symbol	Industry	Current Market Cap		

Date I First Heard About It	Where I first heard about it	Current Price	52 week high	52 week low	Current Dividend Yield

Under-stand the business	Grow-ing or Stable Industry	Intangible Asset Advantage	Moat	Strong Manage-ment	Insiders Are Buying	Recurring Revenue	Growing Earnings	Healthy Cash Position	Can It Weather a Storm?

PE Ratio	PS Ratio	Projected Rate Growth (5 years)			Price 30 days later	Price 60 days later	Price 90 days later	Price 180 days later	Price 1 year later

Notes

Investing Ideas

Company Name			Ticker Symbol			Industry			Current Market Cap		

Date I First Heard About It	Where I first heard about it			Current Price		52 week high	52 week low	Current Dividend Yield

Under-stand the business	Grow-ing or Stable Industry	Intangible Asset Advantage	Moat	Strong Manage-ment	Insiders Are Buying	Recurring Revenue	Growing Earnings	Healthy Cash Position	Can It Weather a Storm?

PE Ratio	PS Ratio	Projected Rate Growth (5 years)			Price 30 days later	Price 60 days later	Price 90 days later	Price 180 days later	Price 1 year later

Notes

Company Name			Ticker Symbol			Industry			Current Market Cap		

Date I First Heard About It	Where I first heard about it			Current Price		52 week high	52 week low	Current Dividend Yield

Under-stand the business	Grow-ing or Stable Industry	Intangible Asset Advantage	Moat	Strong Manage-ment	Insiders Are Buying	Recurring Revenue	Growing Earnings	Healthy Cash Position	Can It Weather a Storm?

PE Ratio	PS Ratio	Projected Rate Growth (5 years)			Price 30 days later	Price 60 days later	Price 90 days later	Price 180 days later	Price 1 year later

Notes

Investing Ideas

Company Name			Ticker Symbol		Industry		Current Market Cap		

Date I First Heard About It	Where I first heard about it			Current Price			52 week high	52 week low	Current Dividend Yield

Understand the business	Growing or Stable Industry	Intangible Asset Advantage	Moat	Strong Management	Insiders Are Buying	Recurring Revenue	Growing Earnings	Healthy Cash Position	Can It Weather a Storm?

PE Ratio	PS Ratio	Projected Rate Growth (5 years)		Price 30 days later	Price 60 days later	Price 90 days later	Price 180 days later	Price 1 year later

Notes

Company Name			Ticker Symbol		Industry		Current Market Cap		

Date I First Heard About It	Where I first heard about it			Current Price			52 week high	52 week low	Current Dividend Yield

Understand the business	Growing or Stable Industry	Intangible Asset Advantage	Moat	Strong Management	Insiders Are Buying	Recurring Revenue	Growing Earnings	Healthy Cash Position	Can It Weather a Storm?

PE Ratio	PS Ratio	Projected Rate Growth (5 years)		Price 30 days later	Price 60 days later	Price 90 days later	Price 180 days later	Price 1 year later

Notes

Investing Ideas

Company Name		Ticker Symbol		Industry			Current Market Cap		

Date I First Heard About It	Where I first heard about it			Current Price			52 week high	52 week low	Current Dividend Yield

Under-stand the business	Grow-ing or Stable Industry	Intangible Asset Advantage	Moat	Strong Manage-ment	Insiders Are Buying	Recurring Revenue	Growing Earnings	Healthy Cash Position	Can It Weather a Storm?

PE Ratio	PS Ratio	Projected Rate Growth (5 years)			Price 30 days later	Price 60 days later	Price 90 days later	Price 180 days later	Price 1 year later

Notes

Company Name		Ticker Symbol		Industry			Current Market Cap		

Date I First Heard About It	Where I first heard about it			Current Price			52 week high	52 week low	Current Dividend Yield

Under-stand the business	Grow-ing or Stable Industry	Intangible Asset Advantage	Moat	Strong Manage-ment	Insiders Are Buying	Recurring Revenue	Growing Earnings	Healthy Cash Position	Can It Weather a Storm?

PE Ratio	PS Ratio	Projected Rate Growth (5 years)			Price 30 days later	Price 60 days later	Price 90 days later	Price 180 days later	Price 1 year later

Notes

Investing Ideas

Company Name			Ticker Symbol		Industry		Current Market Cap		

Date I First Heard About It	Where I first heard about it				Current Price		52 week high	52 week low	Current Dividend Yield

Under-stand the business	Grow-ing or Stable Industry	Intangible Asset Advantage	Moat	Strong Manage-ment	Insiders Are Buying	Recurring Revenue	Growing Earnings	Healthy Cash Position	Can It Weather a Storm?

PE Ratio	PS Ratio	Projected Rate Growth (5 years)			Price 30 days later	Price 60 days later	Price 90 days later	Price 180 days later	Price 1 year later

Notes

Company Name			Ticker Symbol		Industry		Current Market Cap		

Date I First Heard About It	Where I first heard about it				Current Price		52 week high	52 week low	Current Dividend Yield

Under-stand the business	Grow-ing or Stable Industry	Intangible Asset Advantage	Moat	Strong Manage-ment	Insiders Are Buying	Recurring Revenue	Growing Earnings	Healthy Cash Position	Can It Weather a Storm?

PE Ratio	PS Ratio	Projected Rate Growth (5 years)			Price 30 days later	Price 60 days later	Price 90 days later	Price 180 days later	Price 1 year later

Notes

Investing Ideas

Company Name			Ticker Symbol			Industry		Current Market Cap		

Date I First Heard About It	Where I first heard about it			Current Price		52 week high	52 week low	Current Dividend Yield

Under-stand the business	Grow-ing or Stable Industry	Intangible Asset Advantage	Moat	Strong Manage-ment	Insiders Are Buying	Recurring Revenue	Growing Earnings	Healthy Cash Position	Can It Weather a Storm?

PE Ratio	PS Ratio	Projected Rate Growth (5 years)			Price 30 days later	Price 60 days later	Price 90 days later	Price 180 days later	Price 1 year later

Notes

Company Name			Ticker Symbol			Industry		Current Market Cap		

Date I First Heard About It	Where I first heard about it			Current Price		52 week high	52 week low	Current Dividend Yield

Under-stand the business	Grow-ing or Stable Industry	Intangible Asset Advantage	Moat	Strong Manage-ment	Insiders Are Buying	Recurring Revenue	Growing Earnings	Healthy Cash Position	Can It Weather a Storm?

PE Ratio	PS Ratio	Projected Rate Growth (5 years)			Price 30 days later	Price 60 days later	Price 90 days later	Price 180 days later	Price 1 year later

Notes

Investing Ideas

Company Name				Ticker Symbol			Industry		Current Market Cap		

Date I First Heard About It	Where I first heard about it				Current Price		52 week high	52 week low	Current Dividend Yield

Under-stand the business	Grow-ing or Stable Industry	Intangible Asset Advantage	Moat	Strong Manage-ment	Insiders Are Buying	Recurring Revenue	Growing Earnings	Healthy Cash Position	Can It Weather a Storm?

PE Ratio	PS Ratio	Projected Rate Growth (5 years)			Price 30 days later	Price 60 days later	Price 90 days later	Price 180 days later	Price 1 year later

Notes

Company Name				Ticker Symbol			Industry		Current Market Cap		

Date I First Heard About It	Where I first heard about it				Current Price		52 week high	52 week low	Current Dividend Yield

Under-stand the business	Grow-ing or Stable Industry	Intangible Asset Advantage	Moat	Strong Manage-ment	Insiders Are Buying	Recurring Revenue	Growing Earnings	Healthy Cash Position	Can It Weather a Storm?

PE Ratio	PS Ratio	Projected Rate Growth (5 years)			Price 30 days later	Price 60 days later	Price 90 days later	Price 180 days later	Price 1 year later

Notes

Investing Ideas

Company Name			Ticker Symbol			Industry		Current Market Cap		

Date I First Heard About It	Where I first heard about it			Current Price		52 week high	52 week low	Current Dividend Yield

Under-stand the business	Grow-ing or Stable Industry	Intangible Asset Advantage	Moat	Strong Manage-ment	Insiders Are Buying	Recurring Revenue	Growing Earnings	Healthy Cash Position	Can It Weather a Storm?

PE Ratio	PS Ratio	Projected Rate Growth (5 years)		Price 30 days later	Price 60 days later	Price 90 days later	Price 180 days later	Price 1 year later

Notes

Company Name			Ticker Symbol			Industry		Current Market Cap		

Date I First Heard About It	Where I first heard about it			Current Price		52 week high	52 week low	Current Dividend Yield

Under-stand the business	Grow-ing or Stable Industry	Intangible Asset Advantage	Moat	Strong Manage-ment	Insiders Are Buying	Recurring Revenue	Growing Earnings	Healthy Cash Position	Can It Weather a Storm?

PE Ratio	PS Ratio	Projected Rate Growth (5 years)		Price 30 days later	Price 60 days later	Price 90 days later	Price 180 days later	Price 1 year later

Notes

Investing Ideas

Company Name		Ticker Symbol		Industry		Current Market Cap			

Date I First Heard About It	Where I first heard about it			Current Price		52 week high	52 week low	Current Dividend Yield

Under-stand the business	Grow-ing or Stable Industry	Intangible Asset Advantage	Moat	Strong Manage-ment	Insiders Are Buying	Recurring Revenue	Growing Earnings	Healthy Cash Position	Can It Weather a Storm?

PE Ratio	PS Ratio	Projected Rate Growth (5 years)		Price 30 days later	Price 60 days later	Price 90 days later	Price 180 days later	Price 1 year later

Notes

Company Name		Ticker Symbol		Industry		Current Market Cap			

Date I First Heard About It	Where I first heard about it			Current Price		52 week high	52 week low	Current Dividend Yield

Under-stand the business	Grow-ing or Stable Industry	Intangible Asset Advantage	Moat	Strong Manage-ment	Insiders Are Buying	Recurring Revenue	Growing Earnings	Healthy Cash Position	Can It Weather a Storm?

PE Ratio	PS Ratio	Projected Rate Growth (5 years)		Price 30 days later	Price 60 days later	Price 90 days later	Price 180 days later	Price 1 year later

Notes

Investing Ideas

Company Name		Ticker Symbol		Industry		Current Market Cap		

Date I First Heard About It	Where I first heard about it		Current Price	52 week high	52 week low	Current Dividend Yield

Under-stand the business	Grow-ing or Stable Industry	Intangible Asset Advantage	Moat	Strong Manage-ment	Insiders Are Buying	Recurring Revenue	Growing Earnings	Healthy Cash Position	Can It Weather a Storm?

PE Ratio	PS Ratio	Projected Rate Growth (5 years)		Price 30 days later	Price 60 days later	Price 90 days later	Price 180 days later	Price 1 year later

Notes

Company Name		Ticker Symbol		Industry		Current Market Cap		

Date I First Heard About It	Where I first heard about it		Current Price	52 week high	52 week low	Current Dividend Yield

Under-stand the business	Grow-ing or Stable Industry	Intangible Asset Advantage	Moat	Strong Manage-ment	Insiders Are Buying	Recurring Revenue	Growing Earnings	Healthy Cash Position	Can It Weather a Storm?

PE Ratio	PS Ratio	Projected Rate Growth (5 years)		Price 30 days later	Price 60 days later	Price 90 days later	Price 180 days later	Price 1 year later

Notes

Investing Ideas

Company Name		Ticker Symbol		Industry		Current Market Cap		

Date I First Heard About It	Where I first heard about it			Current Price	52 week high	52 week low	Current Dividend Yield

Under-stand the business	Grow-ing or Stable Industry	Intangible Asset Advantage	Moat	Strong Manage-ment	Insiders Are Buying	Recurring Revenue	Growing Earnings	Healthy Cash Position	Can It Weather a Storm?

PE Ratio	PS Ratio	Projected Rate Growth (5 years)		Price 30 days later	Price 60 days later	Price 90 days later	Price 180 days later	Price 1 year later

Notes

Company Name		Ticker Symbol		Industry		Current Market Cap		

Date I First Heard About It	Where I first heard about it			Current Price	52 week high	52 week low	Current Dividend Yield

Under-stand the business	Grow-ing or Stable Industry	Intangible Asset Advantage	Moat	Strong Manage-ment	Insiders Are Buying	Recurring Revenue	Growing Earnings	Healthy Cash Position	Can It Weather a Storm?

PE Ratio	PS Ratio	Projected Rate Growth (5 years)		Price 30 days later	Price 60 days later	Price 90 days later	Price 180 days later	Price 1 year later

Notes

Investing Ideas

Company Name			Ticker Symbol		Industry		Current Market Cap		

Date I First Heard About It	Where I first heard about it			Current Price		52 week high	52 week low	Current Dividend Yield	

Under-stand the business	Grow-ing or Stable Industry	Intangible Asset Advantage	Moat	Strong Manage-ment	Insiders Are Buying	Recurring Revenue	Growing Earnings	Healthy Cash Position	Can It Weather a Storm?

PE Ratio	PS Ratio	Projected Rate Growth (5 years)			Price 30 days later	Price 60 days later	Price 90 days later	Price 180 days later	Price 1 year later

Notes

Company Name			Ticker Symbol		Industry		Current Market Cap		

Date I First Heard About It	Where I first heard about it			Current Price		52 week high	52 week low	Current Dividend Yield	

Under-stand the business	Grow-ing or Stable Industry	Intangible Asset Advantage	Moat	Strong Manage-ment	Insiders Are Buying	Recurring Revenue	Growing Earnings	Healthy Cash Position	Can It Weather a Storm?

PE Ratio	PS Ratio	Projected Rate Growth (5 years)			Price 30 days later	Price 60 days later	Price 90 days later	Price 180 days later	Price 1 year later

Notes

Investing Ideas

Company Name		Ticker Symbol		Industry			Current Market Cap		

Date I First Heard About It	Where I first heard about it			Current Price			52 week high	52 week low	Current Dividend Yield

Under-stand the business	Grow-ing or Stable Industry	Intangible Asset Advantage	Moat	Strong Manage-ment	Insiders Are Buying	Recurring Revenue	Growing Earnings	Healthy Cash Position	Can It Weather a Storm?

PE Ratio	PS Ratio	Projected Rate Growth (5 years)		Price 30 days later	Price 60 days later	Price 90 days later	Price 180 days later	Price 1 year later

Notes

Company Name		Ticker Symbol		Industry			Current Market Cap		

Date I First Heard About It	Where I first heard about it			Current Price			52 week high	52 week low	Current Dividend Yield

Under-stand the business	Grow-ing or Stable Industry	Intangible Asset Advantage	Moat	Strong Manage-ment	Insiders Are Buying	Recurring Revenue	Growing Earnings	Healthy Cash Position	Can It Weather a Storm?

PE Ratio	PS Ratio	Projected Rate Growth (5 years)		Price 30 days later	Price 60 days later	Price 90 days later	Price 180 days later	Price 1 year later

Notes

Investing Ideas

Company Name		Ticker Symbol		Industry		Current Market Cap		

Date I First Heard About It	Where I first heard about it		Current Price	52 week high	52 week low	Current Dividend Yield

Under-stand the business	Grow-ing or Stable Industry	Intangible Asset Advantage	Moat	Strong Manage-ment	Insiders Are Buying	Recurring Revenue	Growing Earnings	Healthy Cash Position	Can It Weather a Storm?

PE Ratio	PS Ratio	Projected Rate Growth (5 years)		Price 30 days later	Price 60 days later	Price 90 days later	Price 180 days later	Price 1 year later

Notes

Company Name		Ticker Symbol		Industry		Current Market Cap		

Date I First Heard About It	Where I first heard about it		Current Price	52 week high	52 week low	Current Dividend Yield

Under-stand the business	Grow-ing or Stable Industry	Intangible Asset Advantage	Moat	Strong Manage-ment	Insiders Are Buying	Recurring Revenue	Growing Earnings	Healthy Cash Position	Can It Weather a Storm?

PE Ratio	PS Ratio	Projected Rate Growth (5 years)		Price 30 days later	Price 60 days later	Price 90 days later	Price 180 days later	Price 1 year later

Notes

Investing Ideas

Company Name		Ticker Symbol		Industry		Current Market Cap		

Date I First Heard About It	Where I first heard about it			Current Price	52 week high	52 week low	Current Dividend Yield

Under-stand the business	Grow-ing or Stable Industry	Intangible Asset Advantage	Moat	Strong Manage-ment	Insiders Are Buying	Recurring Revenue	Growing Earnings	Healthy Cash Position	Can It Weather a Storm?

PE Ratio	PS Ratio	Projected Rate Growth (5 years)		Price 30 days later	Price 60 days later	Price 90 days later	Price 180 days later	Price 1 year later

Notes

Company Name		Ticker Symbol		Industry		Current Market Cap		

Date I First Heard About It	Where I first heard about it			Current Price	52 week high	52 week low	Current Dividend Yield

Under-stand the business	Grow-ing or Stable Industry	Intangible Asset Advantage	Moat	Strong Manage-ment	Insiders Are Buying	Recurring Revenue	Growing Earnings	Healthy Cash Position	Can It Weather a Storm?

PE Ratio	PS Ratio	Projected Rate Growth (5 years)		Price 30 days later	Price 60 days later	Price 90 days later	Price 180 days later	Price 1 year later

Notes

Investing Ideas

Company Name			Ticker Symbol			Industry		Current Market Cap		

Date I First Heard About It	Where I first heard about it			Current Price		52 week high	52 week low	Current Dividend Yield

Under-stand the business	Grow-ing or Stable Industry	Intangible Asset Advantage	Moat	Strong Manage-ment	Insiders Are Buying	Recurring Revenue	Growing Earnings	Healthy Cash Position	Can It Weather a Storm?

PE Ratio	PS Ratio	Projected Rate Growth (5 years)		Price 30 days later	Price 60 days later	Price 90 days later	Price 180 days later	Price 1 year later

Notes

Company Name			Ticker Symbol			Industry		Current Market Cap		

Date I First Heard About It	Where I first heard about it			Current Price		52 week high	52 week low	Current Dividend Yield

Under-stand the business	Grow-ing or Stable Industry	Intangible Asset Advantage	Moat	Strong Manage-ment	Insiders Are Buying	Recurring Revenue	Growing Earnings	Healthy Cash Position	Can It Weather a Storm?

PE Ratio	PS Ratio	Projected Rate Growth (5 years)		Price 30 days later	Price 60 days later	Price 90 days later	Price 180 days later	Price 1 year later

Notes

Investing Ideas

Company Name		Ticker Symbol		Industry		Current Market Cap		

Date I First Heard About It	Where I first heard about it			Current Price	52 week high	52 week low	Current Dividend Yield

Under-stand the business	Grow-ing or Stable Industry	Intangible Asset Advantage	Moat	Strong Manage-ment	Insiders Are Buying	Recurring Revenue	Growing Earnings	Healthy Cash Position	Can It Weather a Storm?

PE Ratio	PS Ratio	Projected Rate Growth (5 years)		Price 30 days later	Price 60 days later	Price 90 days later	Price 180 days later	Price 1 year later

Notes

Company Name		Ticker Symbol		Industry		Current Market Cap		

Date I First Heard About It	Where I first heard about it			Current Price	52 week high	52 week low	Current Dividend Yield

Under-stand the business	Grow-ing or Stable Industry	Intangible Asset Advantage	Moat	Strong Manage-ment	Insiders Are Buying	Recurring Revenue	Growing Earnings	Healthy Cash Position	Can It Weather a Storm?

PE Ratio	PS Ratio	Projected Rate Growth (5 years)		Price 30 days later	Price 60 days later	Price 90 days later	Price 180 days later	Price 1 year later

Notes

Investing Ideas

Company Name		Ticker Symbol		Industry		Current Market Cap		

Date I First Heard About It	Where I first heard about it			Current Price	52 week high	52 week low	Current Dividend Yield

Under-stand the business	Grow-ing or Stable Industry	Intangible Asset Advantage	Moat	Strong Manage-ment	Insiders Are Buying	Recurring Revenue	Growing Earnings	Healthy Cash Position	Can It Weather a Storm?

PE Ratio	PS Ratio	Projected Rate Growth (5 years)			Price 30 days later	Price 60 days later	Price 90 days later	Price 180 days later	Price 1 year later

Notes

Company Name		Ticker Symbol		Industry		Current Market Cap		

Date I First Heard About It	Where I first heard about it			Current Price	52 week high	52 week low	Current Dividend Yield

Under-stand the business	Grow-ing or Stable Industry	Intangible Asset Advantage	Moat	Strong Manage-ment	Insiders Are Buying	Recurring Revenue	Growing Earnings	Healthy Cash Position	Can It Weather a Storm?

PE Ratio	PS Ratio	Projected Rate Growth (5 years)			Price 30 days later	Price 60 days later	Price 90 days later	Price 180 days later	Price 1 year later

Notes

Investing Ideas

Company Name		Ticker Symbol		Industry		Current Market Cap		

Date I First Heard About It	Where I first heard about it			Current Price	52 week high	52 week low	Current Dividend Yield

Under-stand the business	Grow-ing or Stable Industry	Intangible Asset Advantage	Moat	Strong Manage-ment	Insiders Are Buying	Recurring Revenue	Growing Earnings	Healthy Cash Position	Can It Weather a Storm?

PE Ratio	PS Ratio	Projected Rate Growth (5 years)		Price 30 days later	Price 60 days later	Price 90 days later	Price 180 days later	Price 1 year later

Notes

Company Name		Ticker Symbol		Industry		Current Market Cap		

Date I First Heard About It	Where I first heard about it			Current Price	52 week high	52 week low	Current Dividend Yield

Under-stand the business	Grow-ing or Stable Industry	Intangible Asset Advantage	Moat	Strong Manage-ment	Insiders Are Buying	Recurring Revenue	Growing Earnings	Healthy Cash Position	Can It Weather a Storm?

PE Ratio	PS Ratio	Projected Rate Growth (5 years)		Price 30 days later	Price 60 days later	Price 90 days later	Price 180 days later	Price 1 year later

Notes

Investing Ideas

Company Name		Ticker Symbol		Industry			Current Market Cap		

Date I First Heard About It	Where I first heard about it			Current Price			52 week high	52 week low	Current Dividend Yield

Under-stand the business	Grow-ing or Stable Industry	Intangible Asset Advantage	Moat	Strong Manage-ment	Insiders Are Buying	Recurring Revenue	Growing Earnings	Healthy Cash Position	Can It Weather a Storm?

PE Ratio	PS Ratio	Projected Rate Growth (5 years)			Price 30 days later	Price 60 days later	Price 90 days later	Price 180 days later	Price 1 year later

Notes

Company Name		Ticker Symbol		Industry			Current Market Cap		

Date I First Heard About It	Where I first heard about it			Current Price			52 week high	52 week low	Current Dividend Yield

Under-stand the business	Grow-ing or Stable Industry	Intangible Asset Advantage	Moat	Strong Manage-ment	Insiders Are Buying	Recurring Revenue	Growing Earnings	Healthy Cash Position	Can It Weather a Storm?

PE Ratio	PS Ratio	Projected Rate Growth (5 years)			Price 30 days later	Price 60 days later	Price 90 days later	Price 180 days later	Price 1 year later

Notes

Investing Ideas

Company Name		Ticker Symbol			Industry		Current Market Cap		

Date I First Heard About It	Where I first heard about it				Current Price		52 week high	52 week low	Current Dividend Yield

Under-stand the business	Grow-ing or Stable Industry	Intangible Asset Advantage	Moat	Strong Manage-ment	Insiders Are Buying	Recurring Revenue	Growing Earnings	Healthy Cash Position	Can It Weather a Storm?

PE Ratio	PS Ratio	Projected Rate Growth (5 years)			Price 30 days later	Price 60 days later	Price 90 days later	Price 180 days later	Price 1 year later

Notes

Company Name		Ticker Symbol			Industry		Current Market Cap		

Date I First Heard About It	Where I first heard about it				Current Price		52 week high	52 week low	Current Dividend Yield

Under-stand the business	Grow-ing or Stable Industry	Intangible Asset Advantage	Moat	Strong Manage-ment	Insiders Are Buying	Recurring Revenue	Growing Earnings	Healthy Cash Position	Can It Weather a Storm?

PE Ratio	PS Ratio	Projected Rate Growth (5 years)			Price 30 days later	Price 60 days later	Price 90 days later	Price 180 days later	Price 1 year later

Notes

Investing Ideas

Company Name		Ticker Symbol		Industry		Current Market Cap			

Date I First Heard About It	Where I first heard about it			Current Price		52 week high	52 week low	Current Dividend Yield	

Under-stand the business	Grow-ing or Stable Industry	Intangible Asset Advantage	Moat	Strong Manage-ment	Insiders Are Buying	Recurring Revenue	Growing Earnings	Healthy Cash Position	Can It Weather a Storm?

PE Ratio	PS Ratio	Projected Rate Growth (5 years)		Price 30 days later	Price 60 days later	Price 90 days later	Price 180 days later	Price 1 year later	

Notes

Company Name		Ticker Symbol		Industry		Current Market Cap			

Date I First Heard About It	Where I first heard about it			Current Price		52 week high	52 week low	Current Dividend Yield	

Under-stand the business	Grow-ing or Stable Industry	Intangible Asset Advantage	Moat	Strong Manage-ment	Insiders Are Buying	Recurring Revenue	Growing Earnings	Healthy Cash Position	Can It Weather a Storm?

PE Ratio	PS Ratio	Projected Rate Growth (5 years)		Price 30 days later	Price 60 days later	Price 90 days later	Price 180 days later	Price 1 year later	

Notes

Investing Ideas

Company Name			Ticker Symbol		Industry		Current Market Cap		

Date I First Heard About It	Where I first heard about it			Current Price			52 week high	52 week low	Current Dividend Yield

Under-stand the business	Grow-ing or Stable Industry	Intangible Asset Advantage	Moat	Strong Manage-ment	Insiders Are Buying	Recurring Revenue	Growing Earnings	Healthy Cash Position	Can It Weather a Storm?

PE Ratio	PS Ratio	Projected Rate Growth (5 years)			Price 30 days later	Price 60 days later	Price 90 days later	Price 180 days later	Price 1 year later

Notes

Company Name			Ticker Symbol		Industry		Current Market Cap		

Date I First Heard About It	Where I first heard about it			Current Price			52 week high	52 week low	Current Dividend Yield

Under-stand the business	Grow-ing or Stable Industry	Intangible Asset Advantage	Moat	Strong Manage-ment	Insiders Are Buying	Recurring Revenue	Growing Earnings	Healthy Cash Position	Can It Weather a Storm?

PE Ratio	PS Ratio	Projected Rate Growth (5 years)			Price 30 days later	Price 60 days later	Price 90 days later	Price 180 days later	Price 1 year later

Notes

Investing Ideas

Company Name			Ticker Symbol			Industry		Current Market Cap		

Date I First Heard About It	Where I first heard about it			Current Price		52 week high	52 week low	Current Dividend Yield

Under-stand the business	Grow-ing or Stable Industry	Intangible Asset Advantage	Moat	Strong Manage-ment	Insiders Are Buying	Recurring Revenue	Growing Earnings	Healthy Cash Position	Can It Weather a Storm?

PE Ratio	PS Ratio	Projected Rate Growth (5 years)			Price 30 days later	Price 60 days later	Price 90 days later	Price 180 days later	Price 1 year later

Notes

Company Name			Ticker Symbol			Industry		Current Market Cap		

Date I First Heard About It	Where I first heard about it			Current Price		52 week high	52 week low	Current Dividend Yield

Under-stand the business	Grow-ing or Stable Industry	Intangible Asset Advantage	Moat	Strong Manage-ment	Insiders Are Buying	Recurring Revenue	Growing Earnings	Healthy Cash Position	Can It Weather a Storm?

PE Ratio	PS Ratio	Projected Rate Growth (5 years)			Price 30 days later	Price 60 days later	Price 90 days later	Price 180 days later	Price 1 year later

Notes

Investing Ideas

Company Name		Ticker Symbol		Industry		Current Market Cap		

Date I First Heard About It	Where I first heard about it			Current Price	52 week high	52 week low	Current Dividend Yield

Under-stand the business	Grow-ing or Stable Industry	Intangible Asset Advantage	Moat	Strong Manage-ment	Insiders Are Buying	Recurring Revenue	Growing Earnings	Healthy Cash Position	Can It Weather a Storm?

PE Ratio	PS Ratio	Projected Rate Growth (5 years)		Price 30 days later	Price 60 days later	Price 90 days later	Price 180 days later	Price 1 year later

Notes

Company Name		Ticker Symbol		Industry		Current Market Cap		

Date I First Heard About It	Where I first heard about it			Current Price	52 week high	52 week low	Current Dividend Yield

Under-stand the business	Grow-ing or Stable Industry	Intangible Asset Advantage	Moat	Strong Manage-ment	Insiders Are Buying	Recurring Revenue	Growing Earnings	Healthy Cash Position	Can It Weather a Storm?

PE Ratio	PS Ratio	Projected Rate Growth (5 years)		Price 30 days later	Price 60 days later	Price 90 days later	Price 180 days later	Price 1 year later

Notes

Investing Ideas

Company Name			Ticker Symbol			Industry		Current Market Cap		

Date I First Heard About It	Where I first heard about it			Current Price		52 week high	52 week low	Current Dividend Yield

Understand the business	Growing or Stable Industry	Intangible Asset Advantage	Moat	Strong Management	Insiders Are Buying	Recurring Revenue	Growing Earnings	Healthy Cash Position	Can It Weather a Storm?

PE Ratio	PS Ratio	Projected Rate Growth (5 years)		Price 30 days later	Price 60 days later	Price 90 days later	Price 180 days later	Price 1 year later

Notes

Company Name			Ticker Symbol			Industry		Current Market Cap		

Date I First Heard About It	Where I first heard about it			Current Price		52 week high	52 week low	Current Dividend Yield

Understand the business	Growing or Stable Industry	Intangible Asset Advantage	Moat	Strong Management	Insiders Are Buying	Recurring Revenue	Growing Earnings	Healthy Cash Position	Can It Weather a Storm?

PE Ratio	PS Ratio	Projected Rate Growth (5 years)		Price 30 days later	Price 60 days later	Price 90 days later	Price 180 days later	Price 1 year later

Notes

Investing Ideas

Company Name			Ticker Symbol		Industry			Current Market Cap		

Date I First Heard About It	Where I first heard about it			Current Price		52 week high	52 week low	Current Dividend Yield

Under-stand the business	Grow-ing or Stable Industry	Intangible Asset Advantage	Moat	Strong Manage-ment	Insiders Are Buying	Recurring Revenue	Growing Earnings	Healthy Cash Position	Can It Weather a Storm?

PE Ratio	PS Ratio	Projected Rate Growth (5 years)			Price 30 days later	Price 60 days later	Price 90 days later	Price 180 days later	Price 1 year later

Notes

Company Name			Ticker Symbol		Industry			Current Market Cap		

Date I First Heard About It	Where I first heard about it			Current Price		52 week high	52 week low	Current Dividend Yield

Under-stand the business	Grow-ing or Stable Industry	Intangible Asset Advantage	Moat	Strong Manage-ment	Insiders Are Buying	Recurring Revenue	Growing Earnings	Healthy Cash Position	Can It Weather a Storm?

PE Ratio	PS Ratio	Projected Rate Growth (5 years)			Price 30 days later	Price 60 days later	Price 90 days later	Price 180 days later	Price 1 year later

Notes

Investing Ideas

Company Name				Ticker Symbol			Industry		Current Market Cap		

Date I First Heard About It	Where I first heard about it			Current Price	52 week high	52 week low	Current Dividend Yield

Under-stand the business	Grow-ing or Stable Industry	Intangible Asset Advantage	Moat	Strong Manage-ment	Insiders Are Buying	Recurring Revenue	Growing Earnings	Healthy Cash Position	Can It Weather a Storm?

PE Ratio	PS Ratio	Projected Rate Growth (5 years)		Price 30 days later	Price 60 days later	Price 90 days later	Price 180 days later	Price 1 year later

Notes

Company Name				Ticker Symbol			Industry		Current Market Cap		

Date I First Heard About It	Where I first heard about it			Current Price	52 week high	52 week low	Current Dividend Yield

Under-stand the business	Grow-ing or Stable Industry	Intangible Asset Advantage	Moat	Strong Manage-ment	Insiders Are Buying	Recurring Revenue	Growing Earnings	Healthy Cash Position	Can It Weather a Storm?

PE Ratio	PS Ratio	Projected Rate Growth (5 years)		Price 30 days later	Price 60 days later	Price 90 days later	Price 180 days later	Price 1 year later

Notes

Investing Ideas

Company Name			Ticker Symbol		Industry		Current Market Cap		

Date I First Heard About It	Where I first heard about it				Current Price		52 week high	52 week low	Current Dividend Yield

Understand the business	Growing or Stable Industry	Intangible Asset Advantage	Moat	Strong Management	Insiders Are Buying	Recurring Revenue	Growing Earnings	Healthy Cash Position	Can It Weather a Storm?

PE Ratio	PS Ratio	Projected Rate Growth (5 years)			Price 30 days later	Price 60 days later	Price 90 days later	Price 180 days later	Price 1 year later

Notes

Company Name			Ticker Symbol		Industry		Current Market Cap		

Date I First Heard About It	Where I first heard about it				Current Price		52 week high	52 week low	Current Dividend Yield

Understand the business	Growing or Stable Industry	Intangible Asset Advantage	Moat	Strong Management	Insiders Are Buying	Recurring Revenue	Growing Earnings	Healthy Cash Position	Can It Weather a Storm?

PE Ratio	PS Ratio	Projected Rate Growth (5 years)			Price 30 days later	Price 60 days later	Price 90 days later	Price 180 days later	Price 1 year later

Notes

Investing Ideas

Company Name				Ticker Symbol		Industry			Current Market Cap		

Date I First Heard About It		Where I first heard about it				Current Price			52 week high	52 week low	Current Dividend Yield

Under-stand the business	Grow-ing or Stable Industry	Intangible Asset Advantage	Moat	Strong Manage-ment		Insiders Are Buying	Recurring Revenue		Growing Earnings	Healthy Cash Position	Can It Weather a Storm?

PE Ratio	PS Ratio	Projected Rate Growth (5 years)				Price 30 days later	Price 60 days later		Price 90 days later	Price 180 days later	Price 1 year later

Notes

Company Name				Ticker Symbol		Industry			Current Market Cap		

Date I First Heard About It		Where I first heard about it				Current Price			52 week high	52 week low	Current Dividend Yield

Under-stand the business	Grow-ing or Stable Industry	Intangible Asset Advantage	Moat	Strong Manage-ment		Insiders Are Buying	Recurring Revenue		Growing Earnings	Healthy Cash Position	Can It Weather a Storm?

PE Ratio	PS Ratio	Projected Rate Growth (5 years)				Price 30 days later	Price 60 days later		Price 90 days later	Price 180 days later	Price 1 year later

Notes

Investing Ideas

Company Name			Ticker Symbol		Industry		Current Market Cap		

Date I First Heard About It		Where I first heard about it			Current Price	52 week high	52 week low	Current Dividend Yield	

Under-stand the business	Grow-ing or Stable Industry	Intangible Asset Advantage	Moat	Strong Manage-ment	Insiders Are Buying	Recurring Revenue	Growing Earnings	Healthy Cash Position	Can It Weather a Storm?

PE Ratio	PS Ratio	Projected Rate Growth (5 years)			Price 30 days later	Price 60 days later	Price 90 days later	Price 180 days later	Price 1 year later

Notes

Company Name			Ticker Symbol		Industry		Current Market Cap		

Date I First Heard About It		Where I first heard about it			Current Price	52 week high	52 week low	Current Dividend Yield	

Under-stand the business	Grow-ing or Stable Industry	Intangible Asset Advantage	Moat	Strong Manage-ment	Insiders Are Buying	Recurring Revenue	Growing Earnings	Healthy Cash Position	Can It Weather a Storm?

PE Ratio	PS Ratio	Projected Rate Growth (5 years)			Price 30 days later	Price 60 days later	Price 90 days later	Price 180 days later	Price 1 year later

Notes

Investing Ideas

Company Name				Ticker Symbol			Industry		Current Market Cap		

Date I First Heard About It		Where I first heard about it				Current Price		52 week high	52 week low	Current Dividend Yield	

Under-stand the business	Grow-ing or Stable Industry	Intangible Asset Advantage		Moat	Strong Manage-ment	Insiders Are Buying	Recurring Revenue	Growing Earnings	Healthy Cash Position	Can It Weather a Storm?	

PE Ratio	PS Ratio	Projected Rate Growth (5 years)				Price 30 days later	Price 60 days later	Price 90 days later	Price 180 days later	Price 1 year later	

Notes

Company Name				Ticker Symbol			Industry		Current Market Cap		

Date I First Heard About It		Where I first heard about it				Current Price		52 week high	52 week low	Current Dividend Yield	

Under-stand the business	Grow-ing or Stable Industry	Intangible Asset Advantage		Moat	Strong Manage-ment	Insiders Are Buying	Recurring Revenue	Growing Earnings	Healthy Cash Position	Can It Weather a Storm?	

PE Ratio	PS Ratio	Projected Rate Growth (5 years)				Price 30 days later	Price 60 days later	Price 90 days later	Price 180 days later	Price 1 year later	

Notes

Investing Ideas

Company Name			Ticker Symbol		Industry		Current Market Cap		

Date I First Heard About It	Where I first heard about it				Current Price		52 week high	52 week low	Current Dividend Yield

Under-stand the business	Grow-ing or Stable Industry	Intangible Asset Advantage	Moat	Strong Manage-ment	Insiders Are Buying	Recurring Revenue	Growing Earnings	Healthy Cash Position	Can It Weather a Storm?

PE Ratio	PS Ratio	Projected Rate Growth (5 years)			Price 30 days later	Price 60 days later	Price 90 days later	Price 180 days later	Price 1 year later

Notes

Company Name			Ticker Symbol		Industry		Current Market Cap		

Date I First Heard About It	Where I first heard about it				Current Price		52 week high	52 week low	Current Dividend Yield

Under-stand the business	Grow-ing or Stable Industry	Intangible Asset Advantage	Moat	Strong Manage-ment	Insiders Are Buying	Recurring Revenue	Growing Earnings	Healthy Cash Position	Can It Weather a Storm?

PE Ratio	PS Ratio	Projected Rate Growth (5 years)			Price 30 days later	Price 60 days later	Price 90 days later	Price 180 days later	Price 1 year later

Notes

Transaction Logbook

Company Name	Ticker Symbol	Buy/Sell	Number of Shares	Price	Cost Basis	Date of Purchase + Notes

Transaction Logbook

Company Name	Ticker Symbol	Buy/Sell	Number of Shares	Price	Cost Basis	Date of Purchase + Notes

Transaction Logbook

Company Name	Ticker Symbol	Buy/Sell	Number of Shares	Price	Cost Basis	Date of Purchase + Notes

Transaction Logbook

Company Name	Ticker Symbol	Buy/Sell	Number of Shares	Price	Cost Basis	Date of Purchase + Notes

Transaction Logbook

Company Name	Ticker Symbol	Buy/Sell	Number of Shares	Price	Cost Basis	Date of Purchase + Notes

www.ingramcontent.com/pod-product-compliance
Lightning Source LLC
Chambersburg PA
CBHW080552220526
45466CB00010B/3124